A Pictorial Guide to

THE MOUNTAINS OF SNOWDONIA

3. The Eastern Peaks

A Pictorial Guide to

THE MOUNTAINS OF SNOWDONIA

3. The Eastern Peaks

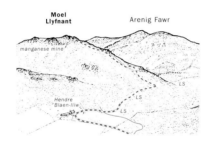

JOHN GILLHAM

FRANCES LINCOLN LIMITED

PUBLISHERS

*To my good friend Ronald Turnbull
for his help and advice*

The author intends to keep this book as up-to-date as possible,
and will offer information updates on his website:
www.johngillham.com

Frances Lincoln Limited
4 Torriano Mews
Torriano Avenue
London NW5 2RZ

*A Pictorial Guide to the Mountains of Snowdonia
Volume 3. The Eastern Peaks*
Copyright © 2011 Frances Lincoln Limited

Text, photographs and 3D sketch maps
copyright © 2011 John Gillham
Edited by Roly Smith
Designed by Jane Havell Associates
First Frances Lincoln edition 2011

John Gillham has asserted his moral right to be
identified as Author of this Work in accordance
with the Copyright, Designs and Patents Act 1988

Contains Ordnance Survey data
© Crown copyright and database right 2010

British Library cataloguing-in-publication data
A catalogue record for this book is available from
the British Library
ISBN 978-0-7112-3135-1
Printed and bound in China
9 8 7 6 5 4 3 2 1

*Frontispiece: Arenig Fawr and Moel Llyfnant seen
across Llyn Gell Gain.
Title page map: Moel Llyfnant Lliw.*

Contents

CONTENTS

CONTENTS

CONTENTS

CONTENTS

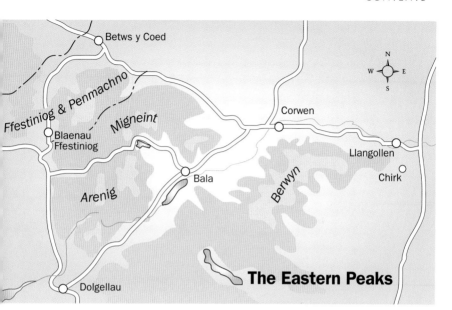

The Eastern Peaks

I'm back in Blaenau Ffestiniog and, as usual, it's raining stair-rods. In the main square a small child is playing on one of the town's monuments, a replica of an old slate train, while his mother struggles with her unruly plastic umbrella which looks as if it will soon be gone with the wind.

Above the town's rooftops, great pyramids of slate slag rear up into the sky as they have done for over two centuries, completely obscuring the mountainsides from where they came. The scene of devastation embarrassed the National Park authorities enough to warrant its exclusion from the national park, so Blaenau remains as an urban island set in the heart of the mountains of Snowdonia.

There's a whistle and a plume of white smoke wafting up to join the clouds as a little narrow-gauge steam train comes chugging by, its red carriages rattling away behind. More slagheaps rise above more terraced housing as I enter Tanygrisiau, Blaenau's next-door village, which is almost built into the rock-faces.

I can see the power station now, on the far shores of a huge reservoir which looks as though the town's thirsty inhabitants have drunk it up. It turns out that the hydro-electric power station – the first pumped storage scheme in Wales – has pumped it up to the higher Stwlan Reservoir. Looking round the corner into the chasm that is Cwmorthin, it's obvious that here too the quarrymen have been at work, but on the climb up the tarred Stwlan Dam access road, the damage is less intrusive and more fascinating. Here are natural rock-faces. On most days you'll see climbers tackling near vertical routes and hear the jangling of their ironmongery. There's a steep pulley incline with a tunnel on top used by some walkers as a quick way to the peaks (despite the danger signs) and a couple of ladder stiles leading over an intermittent wall into a pathless jungle of bracken and dripping moss-fringed outcrops.

At the end of the tarred lane the Stwlan Dam grimaces down on Ffestiniog with a mouthful of reinforced concrete teeth – not a pretty sight at the best of times, but quite menacing on a dismal day like this. Beyond the concrete, the tarn is a good one. Moelwyn Bach on the left is an angular peak with a 'lion's head' crag topping an

Opposite: On the Cwt-y-bugail quarry track with Moel Penamnen ahead.

extensive scree slope. From this angle, the loftier Moelwyn Mawr is a grassy dome. Between them lies Craigysgafn, a rocky arête banded with snow-white quartz affording an entertaining, but very easy, scramble route on to Moelwyn Mawr. This is typical Moelwyn country: savaged by man, but somehow all the more fascinating for it. The Moelwynion, as they are known in the Welsh plural, have the form and presence that override such indignities.

This is the third book of four volumes and covers Eastern Snowdonia – the Ffestiniog Peaks (including the Moelwynion), the Arenig and Migneint lying to their east, and the Berwyn Mountains, which stretch to the Shropshire borderlands.

To the east of the Moelwynion and Ffestiniog hills lies the Migneint, Wales's great moorland desert of heather interspersed with low craggy tors. Seldom does the Migneint drop below a thousand feet. If you hate people you'll love the Migneint, for it's almost a people-free zone where the only sounds you'll hear are the curlew or the raven.

The Arenig peaks are almost as wild but have been tamed a little by the farmer and forester. Arenig Fawr is the highest mountain in the book. Though few people know it, Arenig Fawr's twin peaks can be seen from almost all the high Snowdonian peaks, due to their dominance of their surroundings. Even fewer people will have heard of Dduallt, 'the black heights', an almost two-dimensional peak with crags and buttresses that mimic the top tier of Tryfan.

Lying across Llyn Tegid (Bala Lake) you'll see the Berwyn range. Strictly speaking only the western Berwyn are in Snowdonia but the Berwyn, which rise to 2722ft/830m in the east, are too good to omit. Deep in the heart of their craggy ridges and verdant valleys lies one of Wales's Seven Wonders, the 250ft/76m Pistyll Rhaeadr waterfall.

Volume One of the series covers Northern Snowdonia. Here the 3000ft Carneddau whaleback ridges vie for attention with those of the Glyderau, Wales's most rocky peaks, and Moel Siabod and the Nantgwynant Mountains, perhaps the least walked but the prettiest peaks in Snowdonia.

Volume Two includes Snowdon, the highest and most famous mountain in Wales, along with two not so well known ranges, the Rhinogydd and Eifionydd. The former have been hewn from Cambrian grits older than any of the other Welsh mountains, while the latter have been fashioned by volcanoes and lava flows. Both offer enchanting seldom-trod routes for the connoisseur of fine scenery.

Volume Four will cover Southern Snowdonia – Cadair Idris, the Dyfi Hills, the Aran range and the Hirnant – and here you will be able to walk some of the longest ridges in Wales. In each of the books I will try to cover all the hills and mountains that are of interest to the walker. Some will be famous, others will not.

Opposite: Looking down on the misty waters of Llyn Celyn from Arenig Fach's south slopes.

I've divided the book up into three sections, one for each mountain range. For each mountain I've given various routes to the top, followed by ridge routes to the next peak. This allows readers to devise their own combinations of routes. The routes are numbered within each section, and the corresponding numbers are marked in yellow circles on the location maps at the beginning of each section. At the end of the section for each mountain range I've added a couple of big day-walks – usually, but not always, circular routes. These will take in the best of the mountains and also add some low-level link routes. If there's anything special to watch out for, I've added notes on route-finding in descent. As the routes are less ingrained on the ground than in the other three volumes, due to the remote pathless nature of some of the mountains, there will be more help with descents in this book. **I must stress here that the times and distances given for each route are for ascents (one way) only.**

The panoramic drawings are not to scale and are no substitute for the recommended use of OS Explorer or Harvey maps. In the interests of clarity, I've often raised or lowered a ridge and pulled 'out of sight' detail to the right or left a tad. Artistic licence is my advantage over modern digital imaging: I can see around a bend.

 All the routes are safe for experienced walkers in clement conditions, but in wintry conditions even some of the most innocuous routes become dangerous and may be impassable. If these conditions are possible, take an ice axe and crampons, but first make sure you know how to use them. Be ready to turn around where necessary. There are no real scrambles but routes MA27 on Arenig Fawr and MA37 on Moel Llyfnant would be seriously steep for walking in snow and ice without full winter equipment and skills, as would several routes on the Moelwynion.

Remember, too, even the mountains change. A storm could have brought down a path across loose mountain scree or friable terrain; a bridge could have been washed away by those storms, or operations of some sort or another could have necessitated a diversion or closure of a path. River crossings can become difficult or even impossible after periods of snow or heavy rainfall and conifer plantations are forever changing. Trees reach maturity and whole blocks are felled leaving behind hard-to-follow or diverted footpaths. Always be prepared to adjust your itinerary.

Opposite: In the Clochnant valley above Llandrillo heading for the Berwyn ridge.

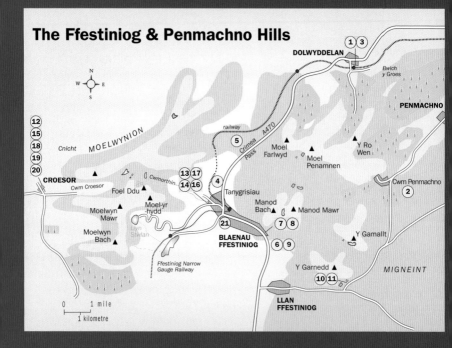

The Ffestiniog & Penmachno Hills

1. The Ffestiniog & Penmachno Hills

The moment you descend from the empty moors of the Crimea Pass above Blaenau Ffestiniog you're confronted by slate; piled high on the mountainside, in the backyards of the slate-built terraced houses of Blaenau and standing like ragged roadside pyramids. When it's wet and shiny and the mountains hide behind a silvery cloak of mist and low cloud it seems the world has turned to monochrome. Every track seems to lead to a slate mine. You can even go underground to visit the Llechwedd Slate caverns – taking a tram down if you like. But the heart of Ffestiniog lies up there on the mountainous horizon.

THE PEAKS

Main Tops	height	
Moelwyn Mawr	2526ft	770m
Moelwyn Bach	2329ft	710m
Manod Mawr	2166ft	661m
Moel-yr-hydd	2125ft	648m
Moel Penamnen	2063ft	629m
Y Ro Wen	1950ft	594m
Y Gamallt	1928ft	588m
Foel Ddu	1905ft	581m
Moel Farlwyd	1893ft	577m
Y Garnedd	1810ft	552m
Manod Bach	1676ft	511m

Encircling the slate town of Blaenau Ffestiniog are the peaks and ridges of Moelwyn and Manod, many with their crags cut into like butchered carcasses. Great forests of spruce and larch fill what would otherwise be fine cwms, while lakes share high plateaux with nineteenth-century mine reservoirs. These mountains are not for the purist, the gloomy of spirit or those who like picture-book landscapes. But all is not lost, for several majestic peaks rise above the scars to soothe the afflicted landscapes and the senses. Those who like to inhale the big air of wide skies, explore quiet corners where ghostly relics of mining mingle with heather and tufty moor grass, will be in their element. If industrial archaeology is your thing, these mountains are for you.

In the north the long ridges are of grass and peat, with sparse surface crags. The deep valleys of Glasgwm and Penmachno are largely afforested. Y Ro Wen lies in the midst of this. A complex of connecting ridges takes you to Moel Penanmen, where a little crag and scree shows through the grasses, then Manod Mawr and Manod Bach. The Manod peaks when seen from the south are fine domes of rock, but get closer and round the back and you can see this is just a façade. They have been devastated. Between the north and south peaks is an active granite and slate quarry echoing to the sound of explosions, busy buzzing dumper trucks and huge lorries carrying their booty down the mountainside.

Across the west side of Blaenau, the Moelwynion fare a little better, largely due to the rhyolitic intrusions that form Craigysgafn and many of the eastern crags and divided the slate into parcels of the lower cwms and Bwlch Cwmorthin. The mining has in the main ceased. These are majestic peaks, angular in outline and with fine rocky ridges and spurs. Perhaps the most fascinating relics are the two great chasms lying near the col between Moel-yr-hydd and Moelwyn Mawr. These are the remains of the original Rhosydd mines, whose roofs collapsed in 1900.

The Moelwynion suffered further indignities in the 1960s. Llyn Stwlan was a lovely mountain tarn set in a glacial corrie beneath the cliffs of Craigysgafn. However, the growing need for quickly generated electricity at peak times led to the building of the Ffestiniog Power Station, a pumped storage scheme. This led to the creation of the Tanygrisiau Reservoir next to the village of the same name and the enlarging of little Llyn Stwlan by the building of a huge concrete dam, a feature that can be seen for many a mile. At off-peak times the water is pumped from the bottom to the top reservoir. The head of water can be released in a flash when required enabling turbines below to produce electricity on demand. This means if you get to Stwlan at breakfast time the little tarn will be forlorn and half-empty.

Blaenau Ffestiniog's growth as a town is inextricably linked to Porthmadog, a new town of the early nineteenth century and brainchild of Philip Madocks. He constructed the Cob, a long causeway across the Glaslyn Estuary, and a port from where slate could be shipped around the world. Previously it was carted from the mountainside to a quay at Maentwrog. The Ffestiniog narrow-gauge railway was completed between the two towns in 1836 and used both as a slate and a passenger train. As the slate industry declined between the two wars the railway became rather

Above: The Moelwynion peaks from across Glaslyn Estuary.

neglected and closed altogether in 1939. However, it was re-opened in 1954 by enthusiasts and runs to this day. Walkers will find Tan-y-bwlch Dduallt and Blaenau stations very useful to their itineraries.

Of the slate mines only the Oakeley, Cwt-y-bugail (Manod) and Llechwedd remain open, although this could change, with our continuing need for new housing. Planning permission was granted which could eventually see the re-opening of the Rhosydd Quarry. Let's hope the planners come to realise the Moelwynion have already suffered enough.

Y Ro Wen, which means the white pebbles, is a great grassy whaleback rising above the conifers of four valleys, the Lledr, Cwm Penamnen, Glasgwm and Cwm Penmachno. Although not spectacular – it has only a smattering of crags – its position makes it a fine viewing platform on itineraries, which could include Moel Penamnen and the twin Manod peaks.

The grassy summit has a small pool and a cairn, while to the south-east the lonely Llyn y Tomla has a wild moorland setting tempered somewhat by the chopped-down spruce trees at the head of Glasgwm. To the north there's a wind shelter, ideal for those seeking refreshment in less than perfect conditions.

Opposite: Carreg Alltrem on the Cwm Penamnen side of Y Ro Wen.
Below: The summit of Y Ro Wen.

Route FP1
Dolwyddelan and Afon Bwlch y Groes

Pleasant streamside woodland followed by
  moorland track to an airy ridge

Start: Railway station car park, Dolwyddelan
  (GR: SH 738522)

Distance: 2½ miles/4km

Height gain: 1510ft/460m

Time: 1¼ hours

Turn left out of the car park and picnic site to the junction by the bridge over the Afon Lledr. Turn left here over the railway bridge and left along a narrow lane (High Street), which passes some cottages. Beyond the cottage of Ty Groes, take the left fork passing in front of a couple more houses before going through a gate, then immediately right over a ladder stile to continue on a meandering stony track signed Tir Gofal (site of a countryside access agreement).

On nearing the banks of the Afon Bwlch y Groes leave the track for a streamside path climbing through pleasant broadleaved woodland. The path emerges to rejoin the stony track where you turn right. The track continues in meandering fashion, now through more open moorland still not far from the stream and the forestry plantation beyond it. Beyond some livestock pens the track crosses the stream – here, you are leaving the right of way marked on the OS map by green dots and following the track heading south from the top corner of the forest.

The surface becomes pleasantly grassy as it zigzags towards the ridge. The view has for some time been dominated by the crags of Moel Siabod, but on reaching the ridge they have opened out to epic proportions, for across the deep afforested hollow of Cwm Penammen, Snowdon and the Glyderau peaks are added to the scene.

The track makes one last curve to the right to reach the shelter on Y Ro Wen's summit.

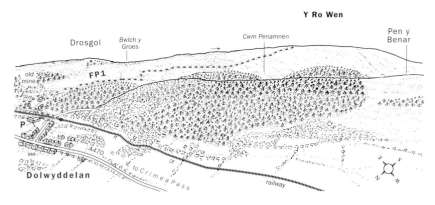

Opposite: The path through the woods above Dolwyddelan on its way to Y Ro Wen.

Route FP2
Cwm Penmachno and Rhiw-bach Quarry

Fascinating industrial trek on old quarry tramways

Start: Cwm Penmachno (GR: SH 753472); parking near recycling bins (but leave room for bus turn-around)

Distance: 4½ miles/7.4km

Height gain: 1475ft/450m

Time: 2½ hours

The Rhiw-bach quarry track, signposted as a footpath from the roadside, climbs southwards, with the gaping hollow of the quarry pit to the right, softened slightly by the conifer plantation behind it. The track winds up towards a long incline, then cuts across right to the other side of it. It now zigzags up the hill slopes past slag heaps and derelict quarry buildings and, by an old breached dam, swings right and enters the forest. It emerges high on the hillside with the chimney of Rhiw-bach and the incline beyond towering above crumbling slate-dressing sheds. Through the buildings on the left you can see the impressive crags of Y Gamallt, while the rounded hill on your right is Y Ro Wen.

The track heads for the chimney, beyond which it climbs towards an incline. The initial sunken approach to the incline is a sunken track, which can be marshy and waterlogged. At such times walk alongside it and to the right until you reach the incline itself. This takes you to the foot of the crags of Manod Mawr's north summit.

Here an old tramway arcs to the right, beneath the cliffs. In a couple of places the tramway has been blasted through the rocks. After turning left wonderful new views are revealed. The distinctive, Ingleborough-like Moel Penamnen leads the eye to Snowdon,

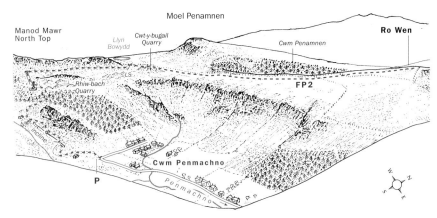

Above: Llyn y Tomla on Y Ro Wen's south ridge.

whose five major summits are all at their magnificent best. Llyn Bowydd comes into view as you reach the ladder stile and gate in a cross-fence.

Here you leave the track and follow that fence to the right, passing the spoil heaps of the original Cwt-y-bugail quarry. This leads the route to the spruce forest at the head of Cwm Penamnen. A faint path continues along the east side of the afforested cwm and eventually eases away to the right, to the summit cairn of Y Ro Wen.

Other route options

The shortest and easiest route tackles Y Ro Wen from the east and starts from the lane straddling the high, afforested ridge between Penmachno and the Lledr Valley (GR 776510). The forest path climbs to Pigyn Esgob, where you climb the craggy Ro Lwyd spur before following the ridge around to the 546m spot height above Bwlch y Groes. The ridge route rounds the deep afforested hollow of Glasgwm to Y Ro Wen's summit. You could also approach it from Cwm Penamnen using the old Roman road, Sarn Helen, which exits the forest at a ladder stile at GR 736478, or from Blaenau using the Ffestiniog Tramway from near the railway station to Llyn Bowydd, beyond which you could follow Route FP2 to the summit.

RIDGE ROUTE

Moel Penamnen
Time: 1¼ hours

A narrow path follows the grassy ridge south for a while then angles right to descend towards Cwm Penamnen's conifers before tracing the forest's top edge. Ladder stiles and gates are in place in all the cross-fences. The path, marshy in places, rounds the head of the cwm to the next summit, Foel-fras. There's no fence or path on the continuing journey across a broad ridge to Moel Penamnen, but as long as conditions are clear, the peak will always figure prominently in views ahead – just head west along the crest.

Below: Climbing past the old quarry beneath Bwlch y Groes.

Moel Penamnen lies aloof from all main roads, hiding behind Moel Farlwyd to the west and the twin Manod peaks to the south, so when you're travelling along the Crimea Pass road or the streets of Blaenau, you'll not see its imposing, Ingleborough-like outline. To the north a complex of grass ridges is divided by the deep afforested valleys of the Afon Hafod-llan and Cwm Penamnen, both of which lead to Dolwyddelan on the road to Betws-y-Coed.

Above: Moel Penamnen pretending to be Ingleborough when seen from near Llyn Bowydd.

As it rises above the 2000ft/610m mark, Moel Penamnen gets a few peak-baggers but you still get that feeling of isolation. Seen from the west it's a shapely peak; more moorland than mountain, but its steep, scree-strewn grass slopes are enhanced by crag and the two small miners' reservoirs of Llynnau Barlwyd, which masquerade as natural mountain tarns.

To the south and west are expansive flat-lands. More miners' reservoirs, Llyn Newydd and Llyn Bowydd, lead the eye to the Manod peaks. The Manod quarry is largely hidden by the grassy façade of Manod Mawr's north peak, but across grasslands the vast scars of the Maen-offeren and Lechwedd quarries lend a steely grey coldness that offends the eye and raises the question: 'Why can't the quarry companies landscape their scars before they leave?'

Route FP3
Dolwyddelan and the North-east Ridge

A rather dull climb but splendid
retrospective views better seen
on a descent

Start: Railway station, Dolwyddelan
    (GR: SH 738522)
Distance: 3¼ miles/5.3km
Height gain: 1540ft/470m
Time: 2 hours

There is a small car park 1 mile /1.5km south along the Penamnen valley lane (GR 737508) but the lane is very narrow and the mile gained would almost certainly be lost on any circular route. So I'll describe the route from the railway station car park at Dolwyddelan.

From the car park go back past the school to the junction with the road, then turn left over the railway bridge. Immediately take the right turn, signed 'archaeological site'. The road passes through the houses of Tan-y-benar. Beyond these it narrows considerably and climbs alongside a stream. You'll pass the ruins of Tai Penamnen, a fifteenth-century cottage enlarged by the Maredudd ap Ieuan, whose family later became the Gwyns of Gwydir Castle. The family moved to the Conwy Valley to be away from the terrifying outlaws who settled at Ysbyty Ifan when the Knights of St John were thrown out.

On the left from here is a prominent rock, Carreg Alltrem, which is a fairly popular climbers' haunt, while the crags of Foel-fras dominate the end of the cwm.

Ignore the left fork to the forestry house, Gwyndy-newydd, but at the next cottage, Tan-y-bwlch, leave the lane for a waymarked

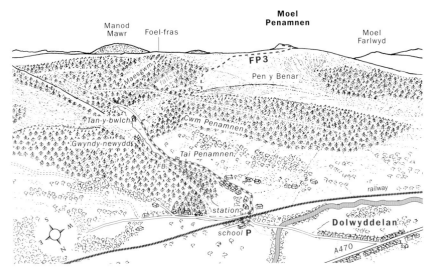

Above: Looking west from Moel Penamnen across Llynnau Barlwyd.

route on the right. This climbs through thickets of gorse, which have proliferated since the felling of conifers on the lower slopes. After forcing its way through them the narrow but clear path crosses a forestry track before climbing steeply through spruce woods on a slaty path, which doubles up as a watercourse after periods of heavy rainfall.

A ladder stile on the forest's perimeter allows access on to the ridge just south of Pen y Benar. Turn left here alongside the top of the forest. A faint track around 20 yards/20m from the fence develops, taking the route though a gateway and over a grassy ridge overlooking the hollow of the infant Afon Maesgwm.

Go over a stile in a cross-fence (GR 718 489) and head south to Moel Penamnen's summit. As you peer down to the twin Bar-

lwyd lakes you'll realise that this mountain has been hiding its best features from you all morning.

Descent

Follow the crest of the ridge north. Once over a stile in a cross-fence (GR 718489) descend the ridge ENE. A faint track leads along the ridge to the forest's upper edge above Cwm Penamnen. After following the forest's perimeter fence towards the summit of Pen y Benar, go though a gateway before turning right to scale a ladder stile into the forest, where a sometimes marshy, sometimes slaty, waymarked path descends to cross a forestry track before forcing its way through thickets of gorse. It comes to a tarred lane opposite Tan-y-bwlch Farm. Turn left along the lane, which leads back to Dolwyddelan.

Route FP4
Lechwedd and Llynnau Barlwyd

An ancient miners' route which in places is fading back into the mountainside

Start: Llyn Ffridd-y-bwlch car park, Blaenau Ffestiniog (GR: SH 696480)

Distance: 3 miles/4.8km

Height gain: 1115ft/340m

Time: 1¼ hours

From the car park return to the main road, then follow it southwards for 300 yards/300m. The track to the hills begins just above Blaenau Ffestiniog's top houses on the east side of the Crimea Pass road and passes an enclosed Hydra works. A ladder stile by a gate gives access to an old miners' path, which tucks under the crags and heather of Cribau's southern end. The path ends at some ruined quarry buildings.

There's no path for a while now, but by aiming for the ramparts of an old quarry pulley house beyond the hollow of the Afon Barlwyd you'll be able to locate the wooden footbridge across that stream, passing a smaller ruin on the way. Note the overgrown streamside mine workings in the craggy gorge to the right. The setting is beautiful in August when the heather is in flower. Moel Penamnen now figures large on the eastern horizon.

Beyond the footbridge turn sharp left to cross a step-stile in a cross-fence into the open-access area. Ignoring the yellow waymarker, which highlights the direction of the old right of way (pathless and rough), follow the fence up the banks on the right to locate a stony reservoir access track leading to the shores of Llynnau Barlwyd, two lakes sandwiched between the crag-interspersed slopes of Moel Farlwyd and Moel Penamnen.

Opposite: The view from the summit of Moel Penamnen to the Manod.

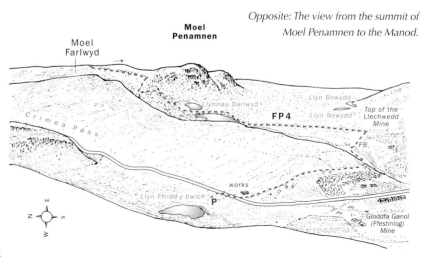

34

From here pass between the reservoirs and climb to the col before turning right along the far side of the fence to climb Penamnen's steep bouldery western slopes. Turn left with the fence but cross it using a gate beyond a fence intersection. Follow the cross-fence before going right over a ladder stile on the ridge-top. An easy grass ridge takes the route south to the summit.

Other route options

A good option would start at Cwm Penmachno and follow Route FP2 to the ladder stile near Llyn Bowydd and the head of Cwm Penamnen. From here it would turn left around the cwm and climb on to Foel-fras, where a broad, slightly marshy, ridge leads to Moel Penamnen's summit. Alternatively you could start at Bertheos 2 miles/3km west of Dolwyddelan and follow the track climbing to the ridge just south of Pen y Benar, where you would join FP3 to the summit.

RIDGE ROUTES

Y Ro Wen

Distance: 3 miles/5km
Height gain: 490ft/150m
Time: 1¼ hours

Head eastwards along the broad grassy ridge to Foel-fras, which overlooks the huge afforested chasm of Cwm Penamnen. Follow the fence around the head of the chasm and up the slopes of Bryn Hafod-fraith. At a fence intersection follow the fence which heads east then north-east to a grassy subsidiary peak overlooking Llyn y Tomla, a small tarn lying to the east. Now follow the fence along the ridge crest to the summit of Y Ro Wen.

Moel Farlwyd

Distance: 1¼ miles/2km
Height gain: 360ft/110m
Time: 40 minutes

Head northwards along the ridge, at first descending slightly left as you approach a cross-fence. Go over a stile in that fence at GR 718489, then turn left over another fence. Follow this fence left then downhill on a bouldery course, with the lakes of Barlwyd beneath you. Stay with the fence as it crosses the gap between the two hills and climbs on to Moel Farlwyd. When you see Farlwyd's crags climb half-right to reach the grassy summit.

MOEL FARLWYD

Moel Farlwyd is a long grassy escarpment rising from the north end of the Crimea Pass to its summit, which just fails to make the 2000ft/600m contour. Although it is largely grassy, angular strata of slaty crag break through in the summit region, as do small patches of scree and boulder on the southern flanks.

The summit, which is topped by a small cairn, looks across the hollow of the two Barlwyd lakes to its higher neighbour, Moel Penamnen and the two Manod peaks, which lie across a grassy plateau and the vast Ffestiniog quarries. To the north-east the afforested valley of the Afon Las descends to the Crimea Pass road near Dolwyddelan.

More often than not walkers visit Moel Farlwyd on a larger itinerary including Moel Penamnen and Manod Mawr, but those with only an hour or two to spend could make the short trip from the Crimea Pass. They would be rewarded with its fine views across to Moel Siabod and the Moelwyn peaks, also the more distant peaks of Snowdon, the Rhinogydd and Cadair Idris.

Below: Moel Farlwyd from above the Crimea Pass.

Route FP5
The Crimea Pass and North Ridge

A straightforward but pathless ride on a grassy whaleback

Start: Forestry car park (GR: SH 706500)
Distance: 1 mile/1.5km
Height gain: 800ft/245m
Time: ¾ hour

Turn left to climb the Crimea Pass Road for the short distance to the top edge of the forest. After going through two gates in wired enclosures, climb the pathless grass hillside to the broad north ridge. There are plenty of sheep-tracks but they're all going the wrong way – in concentric circles straddling the broad ridge.

The tufty grass gets easier as height is gained and there is always the consolation of wonderful views across the pass to the majestic crags of Moel Siabod and the interesting rocky ridges of Yr Arddu and Ysgafell Wen, which lie across field and forest. After a few false summits you arrive on Moel Farlwyd, where a tiny cairn is hardly distinguishable from the outcropping rocks.

Opposite: Climbing Moel Farlwyd's North Ridge above the Lledr valley.

Other route options

It's feasible to use Route FP4 from above Blaenau and the Lechwedd Slate Mines to Llynnau Barlwyd then climb to the col between Moel Farlwyd and Moel Penamnen before climbing left to the summit.

RIDGE ROUTE

Moel Penamnen
Distance: 1¼ miles/2km
Height gain: 525ft/160m
Time: ¼ hour

Descend westwards until you can see an easy way through sparse crag to the fence below and on your right. This will lead across the col between the two hills with the lakes of Barlwyd down on your right. The slopes of Moel Penamnen are bouldery and rough. Turn left with the fence and climb by it, now on grass to an intersection of fences and a ladder stile. Once over it climb south along the ridge-top to the summit.

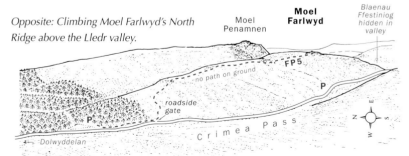

The smaller of the two Manod peaks takes the form of an elongated dome, whose tiered crags, rising from the backyards of Blaenau Ffestiniog, have been disfigured by slate mines and quarries of the nineteenth and twentieth centuries. Spectacular inclines link the town with several mines, which lie to the north of the summit and stretch as far as the Rhiw-bach above the next valley, Cwm Penmachno. It's a scene of devastation with slag heaps, decaying ironmongery and stark quarry faces spread between old miners' reservoirs.

Opposite: Relaxing on Manod Bach and looking to Manod Mawr.
Below: Manod Bach seen across Llyn y Manod.

To the south and east Manod Bach's crag slopes are less spoilt and overlook more rural scenes, with the fields and low moors of Cae Clyd stretching east towards the Teigl and Gamallt valleys and the edge of the Migneint wilderness. Steep slopes, darkened by some heather, plummet into Llyn y Manod, a splendid tarn squeezed into a narrow cwm separating the peak from Manod Mawr.

For all the miners' highways straddling the moorland shelf beneath, no paths have been established to Manod Bach's summit. Happily the way from the north end of Llyn y Manod presents no difficulties. The summit itself has two minor tops, both with small cairns. Both have rough, crusty outcrops jutting from the grassy dome giving walkers accessible perches to view the kingdom of slate which surrounds Blaenau and the Moelwynion.

Route FP6
Cae Clyd and Llyn y Manod

A surprisingly beautiful short outing

Start: Roadside lay-by A470 south of Cae
    Clyd (GR: SH 707437)

Distance: 2 miles/3.3km

Height gain: 1080ft/330m

Time: 1½ hours

A footpath sign and a 'Manod Mawr' mono-
lith highlight the way through tufty grass and
gorse bushes. Ladder stiles are placed at
either side of an old railway line before the
path continues south-east. Beyond the next
stile the path veers half-left and follows a
fence on the left for a short way. Do not cross
the stile in that fence but continue along a
narrow track heading directly for the bold
southern slopes of Manod Mawr.

After going over a couple more stiles, the
path fades for a short way. Keep to the right
of a group of stunted thorn trees beyond
which you come to a firm grassy farm track
(GR 712437) from Cae Du. This leads to an
unnamed ruined farmstead where a waymarker post guides the route uphill to a gate
at the top of the small field. Now the climb
begins with a wall guiding the route towards
the col between Manod Bach and Manod
Mawr.

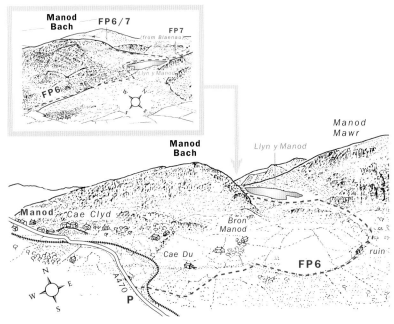

Above: Manod Bach and Llyn y Manod.

On reaching the pass the beautifully situated lake, Llyn y Manod, comes into view, squeezed between the rocky flanks of the two peaks. Go through the gate on the left and follow the path along the western shoreline to the far end. Watch out for a faint path on the left: it climbs past two sheepfolds before fading on the shoulder of Manod Bach.

Now sheep-tracks climb slopes of heather, grass and moss-covered rock slabs. All too soon you reach the cairn on the northern top. There's another on the slightly higher southern top too. From this one you can look across to the fascinating coastline of Tremadog Bay and the Llyn Peninsula framed by the knobbly Rhinog mountains.

Route FP7
Blaenau and Graig-ddu
Climbing up inclines on an urban route to
the tops
Start: Town centre car park (GR: SH 702459)
Distance: 2 miles/3.2km
Height gain: 1015ft/310m
Time: 1¼ hours

From Blaenau Ffestiniog's main car park near the railway station turn left (to the south) down Church Street, which later becomes High Street. After passing Maes y Plas, turn left on a little cul-de-sac lane opposite an old chapel. Go over a stile at the road-end before turning left on to an old mining incline, which climbs beneath the cliffs at the base of Manod Bach's western flanks.

Halfway up, the incline bends right and climbs to a flat area containing the ruins of the old mine buildings. Above are the huge slag heaps of the old Graig-ddu quarries and another incline, while Manod Mawr's main summit fills the skies to their right.

Turn right here to pass a couple of reservoirs and follow a stony miners' track as it climbs gradually to the col between Manod Mawr and Manod Bach, where you are confronted by the beauty of the lake, Llyn y Manod, hemmed in by the two peaks. After going through a kissing gate leave the track for a faint path on the right – you have now joined Route FP6.

The path climbs past two sheepfolds before disappearing into the grasses on the northern shoulder of the hill. Now sheep-tracks guide

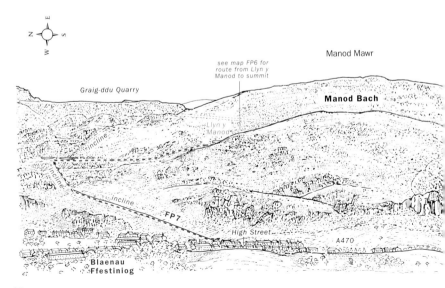

Above: Looking back on Blaenau Ffestiniog and the Moelwyns from the route above Graig-ddu quarry.

you up the slopes of heather, grass and moss-covered rock slabs to reach the cairn on the northern top and onwards to the one on the southern top.

Other route options

The south and west flanks are too steep, which leaves the west face. There are tracks that make a start but they leave you with tall walls to scale and no easy terrain.

LINK ROUTES

There are no ridge routes from Manod Bach as the high land to the north is one gigantic plateau covered with the scars of mining and quarrying. Moel Penamnen and Y Ro Wen lie beyond this, but the routes to them are some-what contrived. Take care, for there are many dangerous mine-shafts in this region. For all routes, return to the Llyn Manod Mawr track. There are ways, mostly trackless and over rough craggy country and through old mines to Llyn Bowydd, where a fence-side route takes you to the head of Cwm Penamnen. Turn left for Moel Penamnen via Foel-fras or right for Y Ro Wen.

MANOD MAWR

Manod Mawr (the big snowdrift) lies side by side with Manod Bach, like two domes. Built from Ffestiniog's characteristic blue slate topping hard granite, its twin summits have been separated by the excavations of the quarry men, to the point where the north top has almost been sliced off.

The slate is also mined in these parts, and there's a network of tunnels deep into the mountainside. The tunnels were used during the Second World War, giving rise to Manod Mawr being known as the Secret Mountain. They were fitted with wood floors and air-conditioning. At the government's behest, priceless art treasures were brought to the bomb-proof mines by lorries then a petrol-driven train, right into the mountain's heart. Strangely, it wasn't until the 1980s, after a long court battle, that the mines were returned to their owners. More recently, granite from the Manod mine was transported to Snowdon for use on the new summit café.

In spite of industrialisation, Manod Mawr's powerful shape and abundant crags have attracted walkers for many years, for the approaches up those steep slopes are quite sporty. The summit's concave slopes shut out much of the mining and offer superb views.

Left: Manod Mawr rises beyond the old Trawsfynydd power station and the Vale of Ffestiniog.

Cwm Teigl to the south remains largely rural, with field, farm and river leading the eye to the soothing landscapes of the Vale of Ffestiniog, beyond which the Rhinogydd and Cadair Idris peaks are framed by the glimmering expanse of Cardigan Bay. Looking west over the summit crags reveals Llyn y Manod, with the smaller dome of Manod Bach partially hiding the magnificent angular rock summits of the Moelwynion.

Opposite: Manod Mawr from the upper Llechwedd mines.

Route FP8
Blaenau and Graig-ddu

Inclines, reservoirs and a craggy route to the summit

Start: Town centre car park (GR: SH 702459)
Distance: 2¼ miles/3.6km
Height gain: 1540ft/470m
Time: 1¼ hours

From Blaenau Ffestiniog's main car park near the railway station turn left (south) down Church Street, which later becomes High Street. After passing Maes y Plas turn left on a little cul-de-sac lane opposite an old chapel. Go over a stile at its terminus and turn left on to an old mining incline, which climbs beneath the cliffs at the base of Manod Bach's western flanks. Halfway up, the incline bends

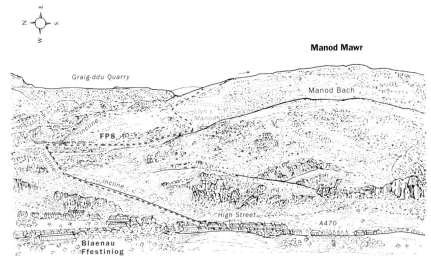

right and climbs to a flat area containing the ruins of the old mine buildings and a couple of reservoirs. Above are the huge slag heaps of the old Graig-ddu quarries and another incline while Manod Mawr's main summit lies to the right.

Turn right by the near shores of the two previously mentioned reservoirs and follow the mine track as it climbs gradually to the col between Manod Mawr and Manod Bach. Here you have your back to the devastation of the mines and are confronted by the beauty of the lake, Llyn y Manod, hemmed in by the two peaks.

Leave the track opposite a kissing gate by the near shore of the lake and scramble up left on pathless stone and grass slopes, keeping to the right of a large crag. This will lead to a low ridge, which in turn leads to the mine track that has raked up from the lake's southern end. Don't follow the track but continue up the slopes in a shallow hollow that is slightly greener than its surroundings. Your direction should be south-east at first, but on reaching the shoulder of the moor veer right to climb south up rough grassland to the shelters and cairns of the summit.

Route FP9

Cae Clyd and Llyn y Manod

A pleasant rural approach

Start: Roadside lay-by A470 south of Cae
   Clyd (GR: SH 707437)

Distance: 2¼ miles/3.4km

Height gain: 1540ft/470m

Time: 1¼ hours

The early part of the route follows unculti-
vated low moorland bordering the farmland
of Cae Clyd. Opposite to the roadside lay-by
a footpath sign and a 'Manod Mawr' mono-
lith show the path climbing slightly through
some gorse bushes to reach the goods railway
line.

Once over the ladder stiles at either side of
the line the path heads south-east, then
beyond another stile goes half-left and follows a fence. Do not cross the stile in that
fence but continue along a narrow right fork

path heading directly for the bold southern
slopes of Manod Mawr.

After going over a couple more stiles the
path fades into the rough grasses. Keep to the
right of a group of stunted thorn trees, beyond
which you come to a firm grassy farm track
(GR 712437), which leads to a ruined farmstead. A waymarker post guides the route
uphill to a gate at the top right-hand corner of
the small field above the ruin. Now the route
climbs towards the col between Manod Bach
and Manod Mawr. It's guided by a drystone
wall all the way to the top and aided by plank
bridges spanning the frequent drainage
ditches.

On reaching the pass follow a faint path
tucking beneath a crag on the right. This in
turn leads to a faint grass track doubling back
right towards a sheepfold beneath the slaty
slopes of Manod Mawr's west flank. From
here a prominent track rakes up those flanks,

Opposite: Manod Mawr from the south-west approach from Cwm Clyd.

Above: Manod Mawr from Llan Ffestiniog.

giving a splendid elevated view of Llyn y Manod and Manod Bach beyond.

As the track nears the great mounds of waste slate lying beyond the lake, take the grassy and less defined right fork track for a few paces before climbing right in a shallow hollow that is slightly greener than its surroundings. This is the start of the climb up Manod Mawr's north ridge. Your direction should be south-east at first. On reaching the shoulder of the moor, where the heather and crags of Y Gamallt come into view, sheeptrods lead steadily south up rough grassland to the shelters and cairns of the summit.

Other route options

Many of the quarries and mines have been excluded from the CROW access land, and this limits the options. The Manod quarry (confusingly re-named Cwt-y-bugail, the name of an older quarry to the north) is still active and present dangers to the casual wanderer approaching from Cwm Teigl, not least from the huge lorries speeding up the tarred highway to the mountainside. The crags of Clogwyn Garw are just too steep and loose to contemplate.

This leaves a rather circuitous route using miners' tracks from Cwm Penmachno past Rhiw-bach and Cwt-y-bugail (the older) quarries (Route FP2) before skirting the west slopes of the north peak from Llyn Bowydd to Llyn y Manod and then following FP8 to the summit.

LINK ROUTES

The active quarries of Manod make high-level routes northwards a little circuitous and contrived. Take care, for there are many dangerous mine-shafts in this region. For all routes return to the Llyn y Manod track. Routes northwards from here are mostly trackless and over rough craggy country and through old mines to Llyn Bowydd, where a fence-side route takes you to the head of Cwm Penamnen. Turn left for Moel Penamnen via Foel-fras or right for Y Ro Wen.

On the edge of the Migneint and high above Cwm Penmachno, Y Gamallt is a squat rocky peak, one of several jutting out from a sea of heather and damp moor grass and mosses. On the west side a line of low cliffs known as Graig Goch (the red crag) overlooks the two lakes of Llynnau Gamallt and a third, Llyn Bryn-du. The mountain's shoulders are straddled by the high road linking Llan Ffestiniog and Ysbyty Ifan. This offers the quickest ascent.

Below: Y Gamallt seen from above Cwm Penmachno.

Y Gamallt has several tops but the highest is capped by a neat cairn. The knobbly ridge is rather akin to the Rhinogydd with its ups and downs, especially when seen from Llyn Bryn-du, where the outlying conical peaklet, Y Clochdy, apes Rhinog Fach.

A vague ridge stretches northwards with two lakes, Llyn y Gors, which ominously means the marsh lake, and Llyn y Frithgraig, which might be a misspelling for Ffriddgraig – the sheepwalk crag. The ridge ends on the quarried slopes leading down to Cwm Penmachno, whose hillslopes have been spoiled by dense plantations of spruce and the barren wastelands of rubble left by the quarrymen.

Seen on a sunny day, Y Gamallt is a friendly place of gleaming rock, colourful heather and sparkling blue lakes. It's a joy to be up there and the views across Cwm Teigl to the Manod and Moelwynion are as fine as those in the opposite direction to the Migneint desert are daunting and mysterious. Seen on a cloudy day, however, the mountain takes on a dark and sinister aura. Storm clouds draw the rosy tint from the heather, cast gloom over the crags and give the squelchy marshland surrounding the lakes an increased malevolence.

Opposite: Climbing to Y Clochdy on the north side of Y Gamallt's ridge.

Route FP10
Llyn Dubach
A high start through fine wild scenery –
    marshy in places
Start: Llyn Dubach (GR: SH 746425)
Distance: 2 miles/3km
Height gain: 620ft/190m
Time: 1 hour

It is quite logical to follow the track first up to Y Garnedd before tackling Y Gamallt (see Route FP11), but for the direct ascent avoiding the worst of the marsh surrounding Llynnau Gamallt turn left up the Ysbyty Ifan road. The fine rocky peak on the right is Cerrig y Leirch; beyond that the massive expanse of the wild Migneint stretches out to the horizon where the Arenig peaks form a backdrop.

After just less than ¾ mile/1km a stony track breaks away to the left. Follow this to its terminus by a small lake. A narrow path now continues northwards with the crags of Y Gamallt lying straight ahead, partially

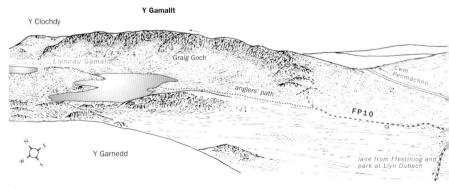

obscured by lower rushy moorland. The path comes to some rocky heather knolls. Leave it here and turn right along the nearside of the knolls – stay this side, as on the other side strength-sapping marshland will greet you.

A thin track soon develops and takes you to the foot of the Graig Goch cliffs, which run the full length of Y Gamallt's west flank. Last time I was here the useful cairns marking this shy path had been kicked over. I rebuilt them but cannot guarantee somebody else might not feel the need to destroy them again.

The path hugs the western edge with fine views across the lakes below and towards the Moelwyn Peaks. After several ups-and-downs you reach the cairn marking the highest summit.

Note: There is a continuing path to the conical outlier, Y Clochdy, with several routes down to the grassy ravine which lies between the two peaks. The first descent to that ravine begins near the west edge and drops steeply between crags on loose scree slopes. The second lies a short way north-east and, although steep, is quite manageable. A couple of others – less steep again – lie further north-east. Once down continue to climb the scree slopes near Y Clochdy's west end to reach the cairned summit.

Other route options

Y Gamallt's rough terrain of thick heather, marshes and mosses means that it doesn't lend itself to too much improvisation in route finding. The most obvious approach is from Cwm Teigl above Ffestiniog. The tarred lane up here is used extensively by the lorries from the Manod (Cwt-y-bugail) quarry. You can leave this at GR 733445 and follow the little path up grass slopes to the craggy knolled ridge above the Afon Gamallt before heading east past the old mine levels and north of Llynnau Gamallt. It would also be feasible to climb on quarry tracks from Cwm Penmachno to Rhiw Bach quarry (Route FP2) before heading south-east on pathless moorland to Llyn Bryn-du, from where you can climb to the summit crags.

LINK ROUTE

Y Garnedd

Distance: 1⅓ miles/2.2km
Height gain: 295ft/90m
Time: 40 minutes

Route 1: Descend to the hollow between Y Gamallt and Y Clochdy then traverse the marshy heather and moss terrain to the north-west of the smaller of the two Gamallt lakes. Follow the faint right of way path through more squelchy terrain to go through a gap in the cross-wall at the west side of the larger lake. Now head directly for the craggy but drier slopes of Y Garnedd and continue to the summit cairn.

Route 2: Descend south along the upper edge of the cliffs, then follow a faint path around the left side of the rocky knolls that line the south-east side of Llynnau Gamallt's larger lake. A fisherman's path cuts across the route. Now aim for a craggy spur that leads all the way up to Y Garnedd's summit.

Opposite: Y Clochdy and Y Gamallt from Llynnau Gamallt.
Above: Y Gamallt and its lakes seen from the Manod with Arenig Fach lying beyond the wild Migneint.

Lying so close to the B road linking Ysbyty Ifan and Llan Ffestiniog, Y Garnedd (the cairns), a craggy and grassy peak on the edge of both the Migneint and the Ffestiniog mountains, hardly makes a destination in itself, but it's a fine appetiser for an infinite number of long days out.

Bound by the shallow moorland vales of the Afon Gam and the Afon Gamallt (surely a historical naming error as Gamallt means the slopes of the Gam), the peak lies in Ffestiniog's 'lake district', where crag-interspersed moors are studded with a host of mine and quarry reservoirs. Llyn Morwynion, the largest, lies immediately to the south-west, while the twin lakes of Llynnau Gamallt shelter in a marshy hollow to the north-east.

The southern flanks of the mountain have been exploited for their slate and the unsightly red scars and abandoned rusting equipment don't make easy viewing for eager eyes, neither do the numerous 'Danger: Keep Out' notices, however pertinent they may be. But such inconveniences are soon forgotten when the myriad lakes gleam like sapphires in the warmth of the sun, and a world of unfrequented mountains lies before you.

Opposite: Y Garnedd from the slopes of the Manod.

Route FP11
Llyn Dubach
A short walk, probably the start of a larger round
Start: Llyn Dubach (GR: SH 746424)
Distance: 1 mile/1.4km
Height gain: 460ft/140m
Time: 40 minutes

From the parking area, walk around to the quarry track running alongside the north side of the lake and beneath the crags of Carreg y Foel-gron. The track bends right beneath the reddish, scarred face of Foel-gron Quarry.

Warning signs proliferate and it is wise not to inspect the mineshafts and pits of the area. The track winds back left, slightly uphill on to the slopes of Y Garnedd. Trace the right side of a fence on a westbound course to gain the grassy ridge and the summit cairn, which overlooks the squarish shoreline of Llyn Morwynion.

Other route options
Route FP11 could be extended by beginning from Llan Ffestiniog village and dropping down on one of the many paths into Cwm Cynfal. A fine riverside walk takes the route past the waterfalls of Rhaeadr Cynfal out on to the B4391. By turning left at the next junction you come to Llyn Dubach. Approaches can also be made from Cwm Teigl (beneath Manod Mawr) and Cwm Penmachno by way of the Rhiw-bach Quarry (Route FP2).

LINK ROUTE

Y Gamallt

Distance: 1⅓ miles/2.2km
Height gain: 410ft/125m
Time: 40 minutes

The problem here is to avoid the worst of the marshland surrounding Llynnau Gamallt. There are two ways to do this.

Route 1: Descend ENE, aiming for the craggy knolls to the south of the lakes. By keeping to the right side of the knolls you should pick up the little path climbing on to the Gamallt ridge to the right of the cliffs of Graig Goch. A narrow path then keeps fairly close to the top of the cliffs. Several ups-and-downs along the ridge eventually lead to the cairn on the highest point.

Route 2: Descend north-east to the left corner of the big lake, passing through a gap in the cross-wall before following the faint right of way northwards. Stay on the left side of the smaller lake before climbing across marshy heath towards a gap between the conical outlier of Y Clochdy and Y Gamallt. A scree path on the right takes the route up to the ridge: if that's too steep there's another path just a little bit further north. Follow the top edge of the cliffs to reach Y Gamallt's summit cairn.

Above: Y Garnedd with the Moelwynion peaks soaring on the horizon.

In the Moelwyn scheme of things Foel Ddu, the bare black hill, is a tiddler, a bit of rock on the end of Moel-yr-hydd. But it's a tiddler with attitude, and when seen from Cwmorthin, it displays a daunting and precipitous rock-face made up of tiered dark bluffs, and screes glowering down on the sullen reservoir. It's a great triangle of rock and, as you would expect, offers exciting views down its precipices.

Seeing how close it lies to the Cwmorthin and Rhosydd quarries and how much rock there is, Foel Ddu had a lucky escape – its crags and precipices remain untouched by the quarryman's pickaxe or his gunpowder. With no direct paths, walkers or scramblers can find their own routes, either with adventurous rock clambers on craggy spurs or through grassy corridors to the top. More often than not it will be a first footer to the higher Moelwyn peaks, but a well-remembered one all the same.

Opposite: Foel Ddu seen from Moel-yr-hydd.

Route FP12
Croesor and Rhosydd
A stimulating route from start to finish
Start: Croesor (GR: SH 631447)
Distance: 3 miles/4.8km
Height gain: 1510ft/460m
Time: 2 hours

From the car park turn left and return to the village crossroads where you should turn left into Cwm Croesor. Go straight on at an intersection of tracks at the road-end by Brynhyfryd farm. Take the next right fork track but just before the next tree-surrounded cottage turn right on a path raking up the hillsides away from the valley-bottom pastures. The lovely little path gives magnificent views across to Cnicht and a steep quarry incline which soars to the craggy head of the cwm.

After passing beneath the slate waste, well beneath Croesor Quarry, the path arcs left to traverse scree runs beneath Moelwyn Mawr's crags to reach the pass of Bwlch Rhosydd not far from the top of that incline. A good quarry road continues east on a flat saddle of land between Cnicht and the Moelwyn peaks.

It soon comes to the ghostly wastelands of Rhosydd Quarry, where the skeletons of the old barracks look across to rusting bogeys and a landscape of discarded slate. Keep the barracks to the left as you pass beneath a mine entrance and incline and look for a wall running up the hillside ahead. Climb the grassy slopes with this wall to your left before

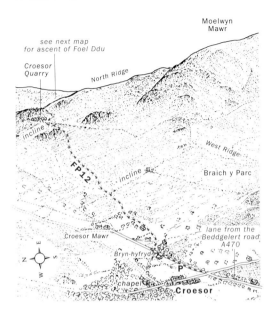

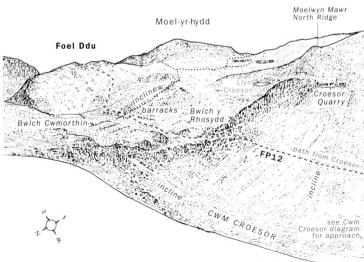

Right: Foel Ddu (left) and Moel-yr-hydd (right) tower above the Rhosydd and Cwmorthin quarries.

passing to the right of a squat rocky bluff with scree running down the lower slope. Now go half-left at the base of a grassy hollow and climb on a rock and grass rib, which will lead to the summit ridge.

Descent

Unless you're a good scrambler, don't try the direct descent down the blunt rocky northern end. Instead head west down grassy slopes, where you'll see a grass and rock rib (note this is not the much steeper and serious north-west ridge, which lies to the right). The rib you're descending declines to a tall wall, which in turn leads the route down to the back of the lower Rhosydd quarry barracks. Here you head westwards down the main quarry track. Fork right on a less-defined track as the route nears the edge of Cwm Croesor (you've gone too far if the main track has veered right) and follow the new track as it rakes down the south side of Cwm Croesor to meet the lane-end at Bryn-hyfryd farm.

Other route options

The mountain could be climbed from Cwmorthin using the main quarry track to Rhosydd Quarry before following a variant using the extremely steep and rocky north-west ridge but this would be far more demanding on the walker.

RIDGE ROUTE

Moel-yr-hydd
Distance: ½ mile/0.7km
Height gain: 245ft/75m
Time: 20 minutes

Descend the grass and crag ridge southwards to the col, with views into Cwmorthin and its lake on the left, then climb on firmer ground on the Cwmorthin side of Moel-yr-hydd's grassy ridge before veering south-east for the summit.

Often disregarded as a subsidiary to the twin Moelwyn peaks, Moel-yr-hydd, the hill of the stag, has its fair share of rock drama. Like its Moelwynion neighbours this conical peak has been savaged by the picks and explosives of the quarrymen and miners, but it's still well worth exploring.

The summit throws out a rocky northern knuckle, Foel Ddu, and an almost as craggy spur which plummets to Cwmorthin's lake. Together they form a sultry hollow above Cwmorthin's decaying miners' chapel. A western ridge overlooking two collapsed caverns leads to Moelwyn Mawr's grassy east ridge.

Just below the ridge the land drops away to Bwlch y Rhosydd, a place dominated by crumbling slate mine buildings and huge slag heaps. If this sounds awful it's not, for the scars are not as devastating as the lower sites and somehow the echoes of the past add historical interest. The mountain is being returned to nature as the blue-grey scars slowly heal beneath mossy and lichenous scabs and the pink flowers of stonecrop.

Moel-yr-hydd's best feature is the south face, where a long line of volcanic rhyolite cliffs, including climbers' favourites Clogwyn yr Oen and Craig yr Wrysgan, overlook the

Opposite: Cwmorthin and Moel-yr-hydd.

terraced cottages of Tanygrisiau. Above these cliffs are the Wrysgan quarries and a huge incline which tunnels into the mountain as it nears the old dressing shed. The reservoir Llyn Wrysgan, now more wild and tangled with rushes, is spectacularly tucked beneath the rocks of Moel-yr-hydd's summit cone.

Route FP13
Tanygrisiau and Llyn y Wrysgan
A sporty route for experienced walkers
Start: Upper car park, Tanygrisiau
  (GR: SH 684453)
Distance: 2 miles/3km
Height gain: 1380ft/420m
Time: 1¼–1½ hours

Once out of the car park go straight across the road to cross the road bridge over the Afon Cwmorthin before turning left on the other side to follow a lane climbing parallel to the river. Where the lane ends, continue along a stony quarry road but leave this for a marked path on the left, which goes over a slate bridge and through some pines before swinging right to a small lake.

After following the lake's southern shores turn left on a stone-built path. This eventually angles right in slate steps towards the Wrysgan quarries. On reaching the ruined quarry buildings you'll see the top of a tunnel on your left. Turn left behind the quarry build-

Moel-yr-hydd

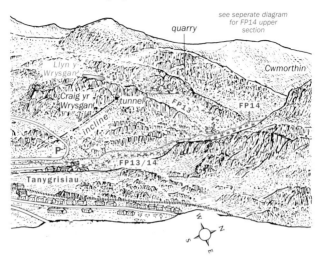

ings, then right on a track that climbs on to an incline.

As you near a break in the incline near to its summit, follow a parallel track to its left, staying clear of the hollow even further left. The route brings you to a grassy shelf of land with the crags of Moel-yr-hydd on your right. Follow the clear path ahead to reach the beautifully sited little quarry reservoir, Llyn y Wrysgan.

A narrow path continues south-westwards beneath Moel-yr-hydd's lower cliffs and a couple of mineshafts. Still staying fairly close to the cliffs, the path veers right towards a col between Moel-yr-hydd and Moelwyn Mawr. The finest route leaves the path at GR 669453 just before the col and just before the last of those cliffs (see picture opposite). Looking to

your right, you'll see a prominent rock face with large scree fans beneath, while to its left the cliffs are lower.

There's a grassy ride between the screes and the two cliffs curving around to a definite gap on the skyline – although there's no path, you can see that this way is a natural climb. Although the last few paces are steep there is little in the way of exposure and you're soon on the ridge. The way you have come gives you an intimate feeling with the mountain and its crags.

On reaching the ridge turn right after hopping the low wire fence and climb on easy grass to the summit.

Opposite: Llyn y Wrysgan seen from the path at the foot of Moel-yr-hydd's cliffs.

Descent

The easiest way is to meet the marked right of way at the col between Moel-yr-hydd and Moelwyn Mawr before following the narrow path beneath the cliffs to Llyn y Wrysgan. Quarry tracks then lead easily down to Cwmorthin.

Route FP14

Tanygrisiau and Cwmorthin

A fine route with a little scrambling if required

Start: Upper car park, Tanygrisiau (GR: SH 684453)

Distance: 1¼ miles/2.8km

Height gain: 1380ft/420m

Time: 1½ hours

From the car park go straight across the road to cross the road bridge over the Afon Cwmorthin before turning left on the other side to follow a lane climbing parallel to the river. Where the lane ends, continue along a stony quarry road, climbing to the shores of Llyn Cwmorthin.

Cross a slate bridge spanning the river to pass beneath Cwmorthin Barracks and continue on the slaty track by the shores of the gaunt lake. At GR 676464 a fence crosses the path. Turn left here and follow the near side of the fence across spongy grassland, with Moel-yr-hydd's craggy spur rearing up to the left. A stream draws closer from the right.

When you come to its banks it's time to climb the previously mentioned craggy spur. This is a splendid stairway up the mountain, and you can tackle it how you like. The crags are smooth and rounded and you could, if you like scrambling, choose whichever of them you feel competent to negotiate, or alternatively you could follow the grassy channels between the crags. At the top of the spur you'll need to climb WSW on steepish grass slopes interspersed with crag to reach Moel-yr-hydd's airy summit.

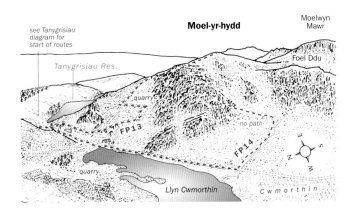

see Tanygrisiau diagram for start of routes

Tanygrisiau Res.

Moel-yr-hydd

Moelwyn Mawr

Foel Ddu

quarry

FP13

FP14

no path

quarry

Llyn Cwmorthin

Cwmorthin

Above: Looking back down from Moel-yr-hydd to the craggy spur used in Route FP14.

Route FP15
Croesor and Rhosydd

*A pleasing route with fine ever-changing
    views*

Start: Croesor (GR: SH 631447)

Distance: 3½ miles/5.6km

Height gain: 1740ft/530m

Time: 2 hours

From the car park turn left and return to the
village crossroads, where you should turn left
into Cwm Croesor. Go straight on at an intersection of tracks at the road-end by Bryn-
hyfryd Farm. Take the next right fork track but
just before the next tree-surrounded cottage
turn right on a path raking up the hillside
away from the valley-bottom pastures.

The lovely little path gives magnificent
views across to Cnicht and a long steep
quarry incline that soars to the craggy head of
the cwm. After passing beneath the slate
waste, well beneath the Croesor Quarry, the
path arcs left to traverse scree runs beneath
Moelwyn Mawr's crags to reach the pass of
Bwlch Rhosydd not far from the top of the
incline. A good quarry road now continues
east on a flat saddle of land between Cnicht
and the Moelwyn peaks. It soon comes to the
desolate Rhosydd Quarry, where the crumbling remains of the barracks are dwarfed by
the craggy mountainsides.

*Left: Cwmorthin Barracks with the crags of
Moel-yr-hydd behind.*

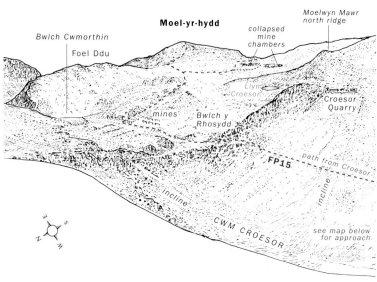

Moel-yr-hydd

Bwlch Cwmorthin

Foel Ddu

collapsed mine chambers

Moelwyn Mawr north ridge

Llyn Croesor

Croesor Quarry

mines

Bwlch y Rhosydd

FP15

path from Croesor

incline

incline

CWM CROESOR

see map below for approach

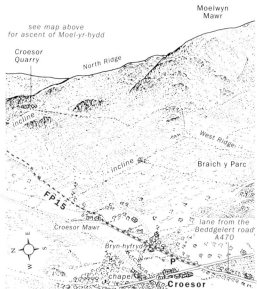

Moelwyn Mawr

see map above for ascent of Moel-yr-hydd

Croesor Quarry

North Ridge

incline

West Ridge

incline

Braich y Parc

FP15

Croesor Mawr

lane from the Beddgelert road A470

Bryn-hyfryd

P

chapel

Croesor

A slate incline just behind the main barracks and to the right of a mine entrance takes the route up between huge pyramids of slate. This was temporarily closed on my last visit (in 2009), and if it remains that way just step off the path and climb the slopes on the left to the top pulley house where the closure ends. At the top pulley house another slate incline bends half-left to more quarry buildings. The track bends right again and will eventually lead to two gigantic collapsed chambers, but halfway along the track you should leave it for a faint grass path on the left, which climbs gently all the way to Moel-yr-hydd's summit.

Other route options

In a variation of Route FP15 you could continue from Rhosydd's upper quarries to the two huge quarry pits before turning left on a grass path to the col between Moel-yr-hydd and Moelwyn Mawr. A simple climb left along the ridge would lead to the summit.

Above: The lower quarry at Rhosydd showing the incline used in Route FP15.

RIDGE ROUTES

Moelwyn Mawr
Distance: 1 mile/1.6km
Height gain: 660ft/200m
Time: ¼ hour

Descend the grassy western slopes to the gate at the col. The grassy east ridge of Moelwyn Mawr now rears up into the sky with the Llyn Stwlan Reservoir and its dam below left. With no fence and not much path to help, gird your loins and breathe deeply before making the simple but steep climb to the summit trig point.

Foel Ddu
Distance: ½ mile/0.7km
Height gain: 66ft/20m
Time: ¼ hour

Descend the pathless grassy northern flanks, keeping to the firmer ground on the Cwm-orthin side before climbing the easy grass slopes to the pyramid which is Foel Ddu.

Moelwyn Mawr – the big white bare hill – is highest of a group of distinctive and impressively dominant mountains looking down on the slates of Tanygrisiau and Blaenau Ffestiniog. The fact that is does still look so impressive is remarkable considering its sides have been disfigured by quarrying on a larger scale than anywhere else in Wales.

To make matters worse, high on the mountain's slopes the mountain's fine little tarn, Llyn Stwlan, has been dammed as part of the Ffestiniog Power Station and Pumped Storage Scheme, which includes the larger Tanygrisiau Reservoir, seen still further down the eastern side, with an ugly power station main building.

But Moelwyn Mawr *does* rise above such things. Tiers of fine crags overlook the rooftops of Tanygrisiau and the peak's distinctive outlines, looking conical from the lower reservoir and powerfully domed from the village, beckon walkers to 'try me'. A serrated, quartz-streaked arête, Craigysgafn, links Moelwyn Mawr with its slightly smaller neighbour, Moelwyn Bach, offering an exhilarating clamber to the stone trig point on the summit.

From the summit, Snowdon, Moel Siabod, the Glyderau, the Rhinogydd and Cadair Idris can all be seen in distant panoramas, but the most impressive scene is the one across the mountain's northern crags and scree to Cnicht, whose steep, scarred sides plunge to the depths of Cwm Croesor, 1,600 feet/ 490m below. In unbroken southern panoramas the skyline includes, in the east, the Berwyn and Aran mountains, while to the west, Cadair Idris leads the eye to the graceful arc of Cardigan Bay. Beyond the Vale of Ffestiniog by the northern reaches of the Harlech Dome is Llyn Trawsfynydd, with its disused nuclear power station on its northern shore.

From the summit Moelwyn Mawr throws out a long grassy ridge separating the verdant fields of Cwm Croesor from the wild hollow of Pant Mawr.

Route FP16
Tanygrisiau and the Stwlan Dam

A tarred service road offers a quick way up
Start: Upper car park, Tanygrisiau
   (GR: SH 683453)
Distance: 2½ miles/4km
Height gain: 1770ft/540m
Time: 1¾–2 hours

Turn left out of the little car park and climb on the service road, with the rushing Cwmorthin stream to your right. The road climbs steadily, turning left beneath the climbers' cliffs of Craig yr Wrysgan and Clogwyn yr Oen.

Opposite: Moelwyn Mawr seen from Bwlch y Rhosydd.

Above: Llyn Stwlan from the Craigysgafn ridge.
Left: The Stwlan Dam.

As it reaches the cliffs of Ceseiliau Moelwyn, the lane begins to wind to keep the gradients small. Still beneath the dam it draws closer to Stwlan's outflow stream and a parallel quarry incline. Leave the lane at GR 669444 near some crumbling buildings and cross the stream on a little bridge, then climb the incline to the Stwlan Dam.

The route squeezes between the dam wall and a crag at the south side of the dam and climbs to Bwlch Stwlan. Turn right on the path climbing the rocky Craigysgafn arête. After dropping to a saddle the path continues on the more grassy southern flanks of Moelwyn Mawr. Almost at the top, the path arcs left and continues along the domed grass summit to the slate-built trig point.

Route FP17
Tanygrisiau and the East Ridge

A challenging start turns into a fascinating ascent

Start: Upper car park, Tanygrisiau
  (GR: SH 683453)

Distance: 2¼ miles/3.5km

Height gain: 1900ft/580m

Time: 1½ hours

Turn left out of the little car park and climb on the service road, with the rushing Cwmorthin stream to your right. The road climbs steadily, turning left beneath the climbers' cliffs of Craig yr Wrysgan. The path marked on the map as ascending diagonally from the reservoir service road up Moelwyn Mawr's east

Moelwyn Mawr

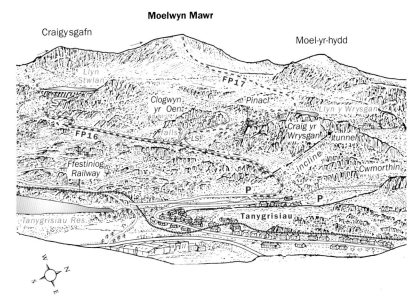

Above: Llyn y Wrysgan.

slopes doesn't exist on the ground, but it's quite rewarding once you've overcome those initial difficulties. There are two routes and both meet beneath the cliffs of Pinacl beneath Llyn y Wrysgan.

The first is a devious route beyond the ladder stile by the waterfalls at GR 676450. This involves climbing by the stream crossing and re-crossing above the falls (avoiding the obvious thick vegetation and crags) and turning right on a narrow grass path heading for the cliffs marked Pinacl.

An alternative avoiding river crossings starts earlier from GR 677451. Here you'll have to pick your way through crag and bracken – on steep slopes at first – and again make for the cliffs of Pinacl.

Both routes now follow the line of crags upwards and soon arrive at a marshy shelf with stone built remnants of quarry buildings ahead, and a small rockbound reservoir, Llyn Wrysgan, to the right. Now a real path begins, passing left beneath Moel-yr-hydd's lower cliffs and a couple of mineshafts. Still staying fairly close to the cliffs, the path veers left to the col between Moel-yr-hydd and Moelwyn Mawr. Turn left up Moelwyn Mawr's steep East Ridge.

Route FP18
Llyn Croesor and the North Ridge

A pleasant route with a sting in the tail
Start: Croesor (GR: SH 631447)
Distance: 2½ miles/4km
Height gain: 2034ft/620m
Time: 1½ hours

Turn left at the crossroads in Croesor village to follow the lane into Cwm Croesor, before taking a right fork at Bryn-hyfryd farm, raking across the slopes of Moelwyn Bank. Beyond the last houses this becomes a fine grassed-over slate track. On reaching Croesor Quarry's ruined barracks, turn right on a track raking up the grassy slopes towards the crags of Moelwyn Mawr's north ridge.

Soon Llyn Croesor comes into view below left and it's time to climb the North Ridge. If required, easier, less rocky ground can be found on the lower grassy flanks to the east of the crest.

The knobbly crags give way to a simpler if steep grass ridge leading to the summit trig point.

Route FP19
Croesor and Braich-y-parc

An enjoyable climb on a fine craggy mountain ridge
Start: Croesor (GR: SH 631447)
Distance: 2¼ miles/3.6km
Height gain: 2000ft/610m
Time: 1½ hours

Turn left out of the car park and go along the lane to the crossroads. Go straight on here on an undulating gated lane heading south across the low slopes of Moelwyn Mawr. The marked right of way shown as starting at GR 636438 is blocked by barbed-wire fences and vegetation as it approaches the Afon Maesgwm stream, but you can pick it up deeper in the cwm by going through the gate north of the road bridge over that stream and continuing along the flinted track.

As the track turns right leave it for a faint path heading NNE to a ladder stile at the foot of the Braich-y-parc spur. The path now climbs the spur to reach a wall, where the spectacle of Cnicht and the huge chasm of Cwm Croesor come into view.

The wall guides the route on to Moelwyn-Mawr's west ridge, a fine if sometimes steep stairway to the summit. There's a rock tower to be rounded on the right and not far above it you'll find yourself looking down Moelwyn Mawr's northern cliffs and screes to the head of Cwm Croesor – it's the mountain's greatest view – and not long after that you should be standing by the summit trig point.

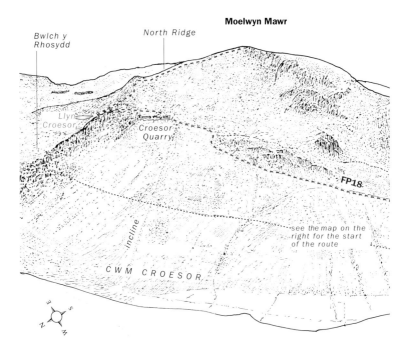

Moelwyn Mawr

Bwlch y Rhosydd

North Ridge

Llyn Croesor

Croesor Quarry

FP18

incline

see the map on the right for the start of the route

C W M   C R O E S O R

Other route options

Brief perusals of the map show there are countless variations to Moelwyn Mawr, although care needs to be taken among the relics of the old mines and quarries. A boggy path, which climbs from the lane heading south from Croesor, can be followed to Bwlch Stwlan before following Route FP16 from there to the summit. Also you could divert off the Braich-y-parc path along the quarry track past Ceseiliau Duon to Bwlch Stwlan and again follow FP16 to the summit.

RIDGE ROUTES

Moel-yr-hydd

Distance: 1 mile/1.6km
Height gain: 280ft/85m
Time: 40 minutes

From the summit trig point head eastwards, keeping well away from the screes to your left, then descend the steep grass slopes of the west ridge. Stay well right of the two collapsed mine chambers keeping to the crest of the connecting ridge. Now climb the simple slopes of Moel-yr-hydd above its southern cliffs to the summit.

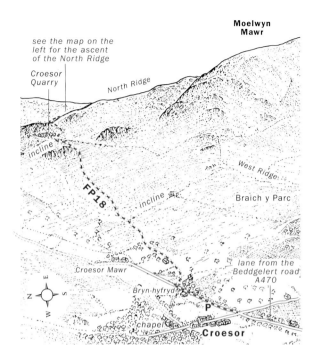

Moelwyn Bach

Distance: ¾ mile/1.2km

Height gain: 460ft/140m

Time: 40 minutes

From the trig point head to the eastern rim of the mountain before descending on a good path down the southern slopes, where a couple of rocky steps lead to the foot of the jagged rocky arête of Craigysgafn. Note the white streaks of quartz among the summit rocks. Below you now are the waters of the Stwlan Reservoir.

There's a steep drop to be negotiated down to Bwlch Stwlan before continuing on a scree path that rakes up the mountainside beneath the summit crags of Moelwyn Bach. Beyond the screes the path climbs south-westwards up grass slopes to a shallow dip between the two highest tops of the mountain. Head west (half-right) to reach the higher north top.

MOELWYN BACH

Slightly lower than Moelwyn Mawr, Moelwyn Bach is none the less a magnificent peak with all its neighbour's fine mountain and maritime panoramas. Less affected by quarrying, its south and west slopes are almost intact and its east flanks recovering nicely from past indignities.

Forestry covers much of the south side above the Vale of Ffestiniog, with splendid deciduous woodland near the valley bottom and conifers on the mid slopes. The little narrow-gauge Ffestiniog Railway traverses the south and east flanks. Walkers could actually get off at Dduallt station and tackle the mountain from there.

The summit consists of two craggy knolls separated by a narrow channel. The precipitous crag face which caps scree slopes plummeting to the great grassy hollow of Pant Mawr in the west has been likened to a lion's head, when seen from the pass of Bwlch Stwlan. The rugged east face has many different facets. More scree slopes slip from the craggy summit rim, almost overflowing down unnamed, splintered crags. Below this the fierce cliffs of Carreg Blaen-llym form a

Left: Moelwyn Bach seen from Llyn y Wrysgan.

craggy spur declining to the south shores of Llyn Stwlan.

Moelwyn Bach sends out a long grassy west ridge down to the Glaslyn estuary. Beyond the high Croesor road this ridge is hidden by the crazed mosaics of farm pastures, woods and rocky knolls which, before the building of Philip Madock's causeway across the estuary, would have been refreshed by the lapping waves of Cardigan Bay.

Route FP20
West Ridge
A pleasant if unspectacular route
Start: Croesor (GR: SH 631447)
Distance: 2½ miles/4km
Height gain: 1870ft/570m
Time: 1½ hours

From the village car park turn left along the lane to the crossroads. Go straight on here on a gated lane climbing southwards. The undulating, gated lane passes through farm pasture, with wonderful views left to the two Moelwyn peaks and the jagged arête of Craigysgafn between them and also to the right, where the pastures fall away to the

Moelwyn Bach

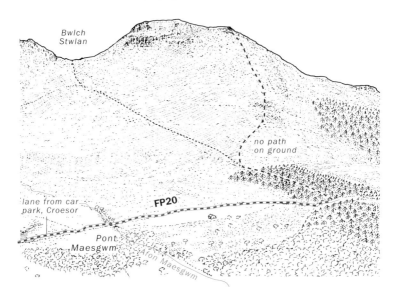

86

Glaslyn estuary. Turn left on a forest track at GR 636435.

At the far end of the small plantation leave the track and head for the drier ground of Moelwyn Bach's west ridge. From here a little path leads steadily up the grassy ridge all the way to the summit. The climb will be remembered for the fine views across the verdant Vale of Ffestiniog towards the heathery crag knolls of the Rhinogydd mountains.

Above: Moelwyn Bach's west ridge with the jagged Craigysgafn arête on the left.

Route FP21

Tanygrisiau and Nant Ddu

A seldom-used route up the eastern slopes

Start: Lower car park, Tanygrisiau – toll
  (GR: SH 685448)

Distance: 2½ miles/4km

Height gain: 2065ft/630m

Time: 2 hours

From the car park follow the lane past the information centre and behind the hydro-electric power station. A stony track continues by the shores of Tanygrisiau Reservoir. A waymarker highlights the required path, which crosses the Ffestiniog Railway before turning south to reach Nant Ddu (the black stream) beneath a canopy of oaks.

After passing through a short tunnel the path climbs by the stream to a wooden foot-bridge. Leave it here and scramble up the pathless steep banks to the right. Head west, parallel to the stream, to a ruined smallhold-ing, beyond which you can see the path, a green swath climbing through bracken and crag. Eventually a wall leads the route to the Stwlan Dam.

The route squeezes between the dam wall and a crag at the south side of the dam and climbs to Bwlch Stwlan, a magnificent pass beneath the rock-faces of Moelwyn Bach and the quartz-streaked rocky arête of Craigys-gafn. Now take the higher of two paths on the left. This rakes across the screes beneath Moelwyn Bach's summit crags before contin-

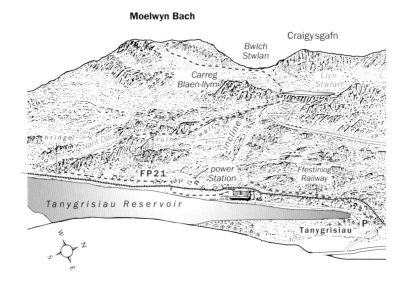

Moelwyn Bach
Craigysgafn
Bwlch Stwlan
Carreg Blaen-llym
Llyn Stwlan
bridge
Nant Ddu
ruin
wall
Incline
FP21
power Station
Ffestiniog Railway
Tanygrisiau Reservoir
Tanygrisiau
P

Above: Moelwyn Bach's craggy north face with Trawsfynydd's old power station and lake behind.

uing south-westwards on grass slopes to arrive at a dip between the two highest tops. From here head west (half-right) to reach the higher northern top.

Other route options

There could be good routes up the steep southern flanks but unfortunately the footpaths that do exist never quite reached the CROW Act access areas, and forest roads don't emerge on to the mountainside. The only realistic variation is to follow Route FP20 to the edge of the forest then follow the path to Bwlch Stwlan where Route FP21 continues to the summit.

RIDGE ROUTE

Moelwyn Mawr

Distance: 3½ mile/1.2km
Height gain: 620ft/190m
Time: ¾ hour

Descend towards the shallow depression between the two Moelwyn tops before continuing to the eastern brow of the hill, where a path descends north-eastwards towards the screes beneath Moelwyn Bach's summit. A scree path then rakes down to Bwlch Stwlan, the deep pass between the two big Moelwynion peaks.

The craggy ridge of Craigysgafn now lies ahead with the Stwlan Reservoir below on the right. Now the path climbs steeply on to the ridge, which narrows into a rocky arête. After descending Craigysgafn's rocks, Moelwyn Mawr beckons and a clear path winds up on rock steps initially then on steep grass slopes to the summit trig point.

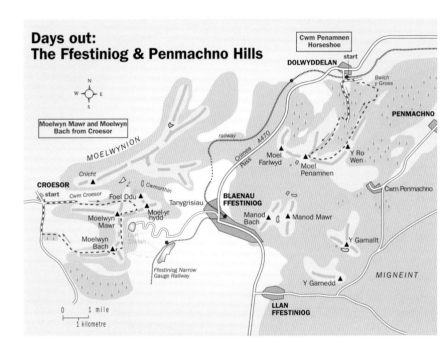

Days out:
The Ffestiniog & Penmachno Hills

Cwm Penamnen
Horseshoe

DOLWYDDELAN start

Bwlch
y Groes

PENMACHNO

Moelwyn Mawr and Moelwyn
Bach from Croesor

MOELWYNION

railway

Crimea
Pass

A470

Moel
Farlwyd

Moel
Penamnen

Y Ro
Wen

Cnicht

Cwmorthin

CROESOR
start Cwm Croesor

Foel Ddu

Moel-yr
-hydd

Tanygrisiau

Moelwyn
Mawr

Moelwyn
Bach

Llyn
Stwlan

BLAENAU
FFESTINIOG

Manod
Bach

Manod Mawr

Cwm Penmachno

Y Gamallt

MIGNEINT

Ffestiniog Narrow
Gauge Railway

Y Garnedd

LLAN
FFESTINIOG

N
W E
S

0   1 mile
1 kilometre

Opposite: Descending Moelwyn Mawr's ridge to Craigysgafn with Moelwyn Bach ahead.

Days out: the Ffestiniog & Penmachno Hills

**Moelwyn Mawr and Moelwyn Bach
from Croesor**

Start: Croesor village car park
  (GR: SH 632447)
Distance: 6¼ miles/10km
Height gain: 2525ft/770m
Time: 4–4½ hours

Croesor is one of the most picturesque villages in Wales, set in rolling green pastures high above the Glaslyn Estuary but overshadowed by Cnicht, the 'Matterhorn of Wales', and the rugged Moelwyn mountains.

Beyond the village the cavernous Cwm Croesor bites deep into those mountains, a mix of the pretty green pastures of the valley floor and the harsh steely grey screes of the mountainsides.

From the crossroads in the village a pleasant lane, lined by hedgerow, leads northwestwards up the cwm. Under the tree-shaded farmhouse of Bryn-hyfryd a right fork track takes the route raking along the hillsides past rowan trees, which offer a splendid foreground to the impressive scree slopes of Cnicht across the valley. Past disused quarry

tips and inclines the route eventually comes to the ruins of the Croesor Mine, which lies in a spectacular position beneath the cliffs and crags near the head of the valley. The continuing track then veers right before straddling a craggy spur and coming to the breached dam of Llyn Croesor.

Most people aim for the lower quarries at Bwlch Cwmorthin, but here we leave them on a pathless course towards the higher quarries of Rhosydd. Go round the south side of the lake, keeping well clear of the marshy surrounds to its shoreline, before climbing over the low shoulder of Moelwyn Mawr's north ridge. Now you should see the quarries and the outlines of the two great collapsed chambers.

Aim for the quarry buildings to the left of these before picking up the path taking you to the left of the quarry pits to the shallow col between Moelwyn Mawr's north-east ridge and the lower pyramid of Moel-yr-hydd. From here climb the north-east ridge, a steady plod mostly on grass, to the stone-built trig point on Moelwyn Mawr's summit. The views across to Cnicht are tremendous with steep scree and rock slopes now on both sides of Cwm Croesor.

There's another mountain to do before the day's done, so don't succumb to the urge to linger longer than lunchtime. Retrace your steps east for around 100yds/m before descending south to tackle the jagged quartz-banded ridge of Craigysgafn. In places the ridge is a bit of a scramble but never frightening or exposed. Down below and on your left is Llyn Stwlan, part of the Ffestiniog Pumped Storage Scheme. If it's empty, the water has been tipped into the larger Tanygrisiau Reservoir in the valley.

At the narrow pass of Bwlch Stwlan you're confronted by the impressive crags and great screes of Moelwyn Bach. To the left of the lion-like rock barring any thoughts of a direct ascent is a path raking across the screes: this should not be confused with the larger track nearer the base of the screes. Following this fine path brings you to a shallow grass hollow just to the south of the summit. By climbing half-right you'll get to the top.

Moelwyn Bach throws out a splendid west ridge, grassy and with easy gradients. As you descend, the late afternoon sun (if you're lucky enough) should be glinting on the waves of Tremadog Bay framed by the Eifionydd peaks and the Llyn Peninsula. It's a glorious end to the day.

On nearing the bottom of the ridge break off half-right for the right-hand corner of a small conifer plantation. Through a gate a forest path leads to a high lane. Turn right along this undulating gated lane, which returns to the crossroads in Croesor village.

Opposite: Y Ro Wen seen from Foel-fras and across Cwm Penamnen.

The Cwm Penamnen Horseshoe

Start: Station car park, Dolwyddelan
  (GR: SH 738522)

Distance: 8¾ miles/14.2km

Height gain: 2165ft/660m

Time: 4–5 hours

Cwm Penamnen has been filled to the ridges with spruce and larch plantations, and it's hard to believe at first glance that this is a place of history. It's a place where the Romans marched along their Sarn Helen road on forays across the high mountains to Tomen y Mur (Trawsfynydd). The road would also have been used in subsequent centuries by the likes of Prince Llewelyn the Great, who built the castle at Dolwyddelan.

The car park by the railway is ideal as the starting point for exploration as it lies at the mouth of the valley. Not long after crossing the railway and passing through the row of cottages, a little gated lane accompanies the lively stream through the valley. Soon a huge crag on the hillside to the left comes into view. This is Carreg Alltrem, which is a fairly popular climbers' haunt.

On the right are the ruins of Tai Penamnen, built during the Wars of the Roses and enlarged by the Maredudd ap Ieuan, whose family later became the Gwyns of Gwydir Castle. It has been suggested that they moved to the Conwy Valley to be away from the outlaws who settled in the valley at Ysbyty Ifan when the Knights of St John were thrown out.

A steep, waymarked right of way opposite Tan-y-bwlch farm takes the route through conifers old and new, crossing a forestry track en route to the Penamnen ridge. At first the route traces the upper edge of the forest but, confronted by the hollow of the Afon Maesgwm, a faint track climbs along a broad grassy ridge. The stile to be crossed in the fence lies close to the fence intersection at GR 717490.

From there the route heads south on grass to Moel Penamnen's summit. Detour to the western edge to view the mountain's crags and the twin Barlwyd lakes. Looking west and south the mountainscapes are scattered with the relics of slate quarrying, including two more reservoirs, Llyn Bowydd and Llyn Newydd, which lie beneath the crags of Manod Mawr's northern top.

Now we head east on a broad marshy ridge to the rounded grassy summit of Foelfras. From here a fence leads around the head of Cwm Penamnen where you can review most of the day's walk beneath your feet. Sarn Helen comes up to meet you as you round the eastern side of the cwm, but it's not easily discernible on the plateau. Around here you can look down into another valley on the right, Cwm Penmachno, where the hillsides are fringed with the crags of Blaen-y-cwm.

As the bulk of Y Ro Wen looms, the faint path eases away right (north-east) from the forest to climb to its summit, where there's a cairn and shelter. Moel Siabod looks absolutely magnificent in views to the north, where its rocky cwm and the spur of Daear Ddu overlook the tiny houses of Dolwyddelan.

A farm track continues northwards but leave it when it starts to descend left of the ridge. This route stays on the ridge until Bwlch y Groes where it turns left on an intermittent path, which used to be a traders' route between Dolwyddelan and Penmachno. The track you left is rejoined further downhill but in the interests of a pleasant route it is once again abandoned for a woodland path down left (GR 741519). The path follows a stream down to a gate by the highest of Pentre-bont's cottages.

Beyond this a lane leads down to a junction where you turn left, then right over the bridge spanning the railway. Another right turn leads back to the car park.

Opposite: Approaching the summit of Y Ro Wen.

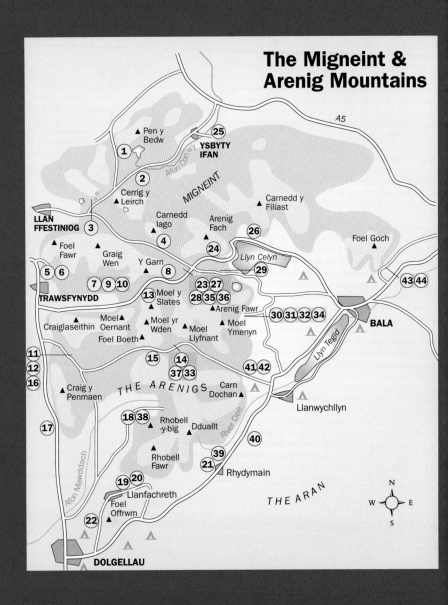

The Migneint & Arenig Mountains

A5

▲ Pen y Bedw

① ②⑤ YSBYTY IFAN

Afon Conwy

② MIGNEINT

▲ Cerrig y Leirch

▲ Carnedd y Filiast

LLAN FFESTINIOG ③

▲ Carnedd Iago

④ Arenig Fach ▲ ②④

②⑥ Foel Goch ▲

▲ Foel Fawr

▲ Graig Wen

Y Garn ▲ ⑧

②⑥ Llyn Celyn ②⑨

⑤ ⑥

⑦ ⑨ ⑩

TRAWSFYNYDD ⑬ Moel y Slates

②③②⑦ ②⑧③⑤③⑥

▲ Arenig Fawr

③⓪③①③②③④ BALA

Craiglaseithin ▲ Moel▲ Oernant ▲ Moel yr Wden Moel ▲ Llyfnant

Moel Ymenyn ▲

▲ Foel Boeth

⑪ ⑫ ⑯

⑮ ⑭

③⑦③③

④①④②

Llyn Tegid

THE ARENIGS

Carn Dochan ▲

▲ Craig y Penmaen

Llanwychllyn

⑰

⑱③⑧ Rhobell -y-big Dduallt ▲

River Dee

④⓪

Rhobell Fawr ▲

③⑨ ④①

Rhydymain ▲

⑲②⓪ Llanfachreth

THE ARAN

Foel Offrwm ▲

②②

N
W ✦ E
S

DOLGELLAU

A little lane climbs out of Bronaber south of Trawsfynydd's great lake and takes you past holiday chalets into a surprising landscape where golden-coloured, seldom-trodden hills are spread before you. After some exploration you see a few unexplainable things.

On the roadside near an old chapel there's a concrete bus shelter with dustbins in it, something that looks like a kiln, several iron sheet piles driven into the ground. This is remote countryside, what can it mean? Well, from 1906 until 1958 there was a military camp based on the holiday chalet site. The bus shelter was a sentry box, the kiln a look-out post, and those piles were the bases of flag-poles. The hills were part of a huge firing range where young soldiers trained for both world wars.

Soldiers were here long before this, however. The Roman road, Sarn Helen, straddled these moors linking forts at Conwy (Caerhun) with Brecon (Y Gaer). You can see the remains of a Roman amphitheatre at Tomen-y-mur and prac-

THE PEAKS

Main Tops	height	
Arenig Fawr	2801ft	854m
Moel Llyfnant	2464ft	751m
Rhobell Fawr	2408ft	734m
Arenig Fach	2259ft	689m
Carnedd y Filiast	2171ft	669m
Dduallt	2155ft	662m
Foel Boeth		
(Gallt y Daren)	2030ft	619m
Foel Goch	2004ft	611m
Moel yr Wden	1853ft	565m
Graig Wen	1823ft	556m
Moel Ymenyn	1804ft	550m
Carnedd Iago	1764ft	538m
Pen y Bedw (east top)	1731ft	528m
Foel Fawr	1731ft	528m
Cerrig y Leirch	1682ft	513m
Rhobell-y-big	1653ft	504m
Moel Oernant	1649ft	503m
Y Garn (Craig Aderyn)	1554ft	474m
Craiglaseithin	1528ft	466m
Craig Penmaen	1377ft	420m
Foel Offrwm	1328ft	405m
Carn Dochan	1102ft	336m

Above: Migneint blanket bog.

tice works at Dolddinas en route to places like Graig Wen, a remote hill overlooking Llan Ffestiniog's Cwm Cynfal and Y Garn above Cwm Prysor.

To the east of all this lies the Migneint, which means swampy place, a vast tract of high, desolate plateau, the principality's largest and most important wilderness. It's made up of blanket bog, heath and rough grass moor, traversed by no major roads, ideal for the curlews, wheatears and snipe who nest here.

The area as a whole is bound by three rivers, the Conwy, Gelyn and Tryweryn, and reaches its highest point on the summit of Arenig Fach (2259ft/689m). The Afon Serw cuts through the middle, forming one of the most rugged little valleys in Snowdonia.

Close inspection of the terrain reveals a host of colours: the reds and bright greens of the mosses, the biscuit-coloured tufty grasses, and the dark cocoa of the dormant heather. The terrain is wide and wonderful; plateau-like, as if a blanket had been roughly spread out beneath your feet. In distant views, and when it's caught by the sun's rays, the blanket becomes a weave of russets and golden beige dotted with the bright blue of distant lakes.

Perhaps the most romantic of these is Llyn Serw, at the head of the previously mentioned valley. Not far from here Cefngarw, the remotest of farm cottages, can be seen for miles. The Migneint can be marshy, dangerously confusing in mist and unrelenting in its harshness. But choose to explore this wonderland on a fine day and you'll be rewarded by a spaciousness seldom seen elsewhere, an endearing simplicity of landscape, and a freedom to roam that the combination of those two things allows.

On the edges of the Migneint the Conwy is born in a large lake, Llyn Conwy, which lies high on the heather slopes of Pen y Bedw. It was once owned by the Knights of St John of Jerusalem who had a preceptory at Ysbyty Ifan a few miles further down the valley. More can be learned of this by visiting the church, which now stands on the site of their hospice. The order was consumed by corruption and at the time of the dissolution of the monasteries was little more than a den of thieves who terrorised the local population. Ysbyty Ifan became an important crossroads for drovers who would herd cattle to the markets of England and pilgrims en route to Bardsey Island and Anglesey. The drove roads provide excellent ways into the hills, especially to Carnedd y Filiast, Arenig Fach and Gylchedd.

The Afon Prysor flows lazily from the tussocks of the foothills of the Arenig, through the pastures of Cwm Prysor into Llyn Trawsfynydd, beyond whose dam it picks up speed and enthusiasm to plummet through the trees in torrents of white water before emptying into the Ffestiniog Valley's Afon Dwyryd near Maentwrog.

Two hills are sandwiched between this river at Cwm Prysor and the Afon Gain a little way south. One, Craiglaseithin, has a distinctive craggy profile, while the other, Moel Oernant, is rather more rounded. Both offer a splendid round for those who like their hills remote and peaceful. Llyn Gelli Gain promises little but, when seen on a bright, crisp autumn day when the vegetation wears a fiery glow, this place is quite magnificent with the surrounding crags acting as a perfect foil for the peaks of Arenig Fawr and Moel Llyfnant in the background.

These days the Tryweryn Valley, which lies on the east side of a moorland col from Cwm Prysor, has been tamed by forestry and by the fast A4212 road from Bala to Trawsfynydd, but in the 1950s it was almost as remote as the Migneint. There was one small village, Capel Tryweryn, a small, tightly knit, Welsh-speaking community. Liverpool needed water and their engineers turned to the valley. In spite of vehement opposition a bill was passed. Capel Tryweryn was inundated, the railway which ran through the valley was closed, and the rich pastures submerged by a rising wall of water. The opening ceremony was curtailed after three minutes when protestors cut the microphone wires, and in 2005 Liverpool council apologised to the people of Wales for its part. It has been suggested that the whole affair was the catalyst for the rise of Plaid Cymru, the Welsh Nationalist Party.

While the railway from Bala to Blaenau Ffestiniog was closed to make way for Llyn Celyn, its trackbed is still useful for walkers. The old Arenig station forms a car park for Arenig Fawr, and further west walkers can cross an impressive viaduct and cut across a quarried rock-face on their way to a heather and rock peak called Y Garn. This peak has a splendidly shaped large lake just below the summit.

Llyn Celyn is shaded by the huge northern crags of Arenig Fawr, the area's highest mountain at over 2800 feet/850m. Arenig has true majesty. Its twin peaks can be seen for miles around and most of the Snowdonian peaks can be seen from its summit. It's a friendly giant, though – you can almost make your own routes to the top once you're into the access area. The mountain has a wide crag-ringed corrie to the east accommodating the enlarged corrie lake, Llyn Arenig Fawr. The track to here provides the most popular route to the top.

Very much overshadowed by its eastern neighbour Arenig Fawr in both height and mountain architecture, Moel Llyfnant is still a fine 2000ft/600m peak. In fact, when seen from the Lliw Valley, Moel Llyfnant may appear Arenig Fawr's equal, with a superior cone-like outline and steep slopes scraped by scree and crusty crags. When you look south from the summit, views of unfamiliar peaks whet the appetite for further exploration.

Across the Lliw Valley some rugged crags lead the eye across sombre moorland, almost as wild as the Migneint. Standing proud of this moorland shelf are the dark crags and buttresses known as Dduallt, the black heights. Dduallt looks like the top quarter of Tryfan with everything below Heather Terrace submerged beneath the moor. And that moor, known as Waun y Griafolen, gives birth to two of Wales's great rivers, the Mawddach, which flows into Cardigan Bay at Barmouth, and the Dee, which after passing through Bala and Chester forms a great industrial estuary south of the Wirral.

Behind Dduallt lies Rhobell Fawr, a mountain of great girth studded with knobbly volcanic crags interspersed with grass which is surprisingly easy to walk on, and not of the tussocky kind experienced on many high hills. One person who would have been thankful for this would have been St Machreth, a fifth-century Irish missionary,

Above: Arenig Fawr from the north-east.

who is said to have retreated to a cave in the mountain. The charming village of Llan-fachreth, which lies on the mountain's southern slopes, was named after him.

To the west Rhobell Fawr's slopes are submerged by the inky plantations of Coed y Brenin, the king's forest. Deep in these forests the Mawddach and Gain rivers form attractive waterfalls, but they're most famous for gold mines, which flourished in past centuries but sadly lie dormant and decaying. Today the area is better known for the excellent network of mountain bike routes.

The last outposts of the Arenig, all of which overlook the pastoral valley of the Afon Wnion, are peaks in miniature, and they have an interesting history. The furthest east is Carn Dochan, named Castell Carndochan on the map, referring to the ancient fort, which stands ruinous but still very evident on the summit. This peak is guarded on three sides by powerful crags and is without doubt the most splendid short walk in the book.

There's another fort on Foel Offrwm, which also has wonderful views of Cadair Idris across the wide valley of the Mawddach. Foel Offrwm also looks across to the twin peaks of Foel Cynwch and Foel Faner, known to the many tourists who walk around their high slopes as part of the famous Precipice Walk.

Overleaf: The Ffestiniog hills seen from the slopes of Graig Fawr in the Arenig.

PEN Y BEDW

At Pen y Bedw, the hill of birches, the great Migneint meets the fresh green fields and the conifer forests of Cwm Penmachno, where sombre wilderness meets the world of human endeavour. The Penmachno sides are steep and straight, with no river ravines or cwms. Atop them are two rounded summits clad with short-cropped heather.

There has been debate which one of these summits is the higher, east or west? The Ordnance Survey had the west top marked as 527m and the east top unmarked, while Harveys had the east top as 528m. I would have preferred the cairned west top to come out first but recently surveyors Graham Jackson and Myrddyn Phillips have concluded that the east top is indeed a half-metre higher.

A narrow lane winds up out of Cwm Penmachno before wending its way across the Migneint plateau, and it is from here that the mountain is usually climbed. From this direction the mountain appears squat, with gracefully curved twin peaks rising just high enough from an ocean of heather to be of interest to the walker. The heather is quite thick and tangly though, and walkers would be advised not to stray too far off the narrow peaty trods which criss-cross the moor.

Left: Llyn Conwy with Pen y Bedw behind.

They will soon come across an expansive lake, Llyn Conwy, which at 1492ft/455m above sea level is the source of the Afon Conwy, the great river that flows out to the Irish Sea beneath the castle of the same name and Llandudno's Great Orme. Although a natural lake, it is used as a reservoir and by anglers (including at one time Lord Penrhyn), who come to fish for the trout.

Walkers who enjoy wilderness and solitude will love Pen y Bedw; others may find the patches of blanket bog surrounding the lake a little too much of a toil. I belong to the former group.

Route MA1
Cwm Hafodyredwydd

A rough walk with fine views across the wild Migneint Moors

Start: Off-lane car parking by Hafodyredwydd (GR: SH 765457)

Distance: 2 miles/3.2km

Height gain: 525ft/160m

Time: 1¼ hours

Strangely the old wooden footpath signpost at GR 765457 is incorrectly sited. Walk a few paces towards the cottage of Hafodyredwydd and follow the grassy track to the east. This old track is filled with rushes and you find yourself walking on a raised grassy bank beside it. Views northwards into Cwm Hafodyredwydd and Cwm Penmachno are pleasant, but made a little sombre by the larch and

spruce trees cloaking the lower hillslopes.

The track comes to a stream on the left (GR 767460), which has cut a little rocky gorge. Here it veers right (ESE) to follow the stream, which soon becomes shallow and its bed wide and rush-filled. On reaching a cross-fence turn left, still on a grassy raised bank running parallel to the fence. Go across a ladder stile (GR 770461) and turn right on a faint track for a few paces to locate a similarly narrow trod that climbs eastwards across heather moorland. Suddenly the massive expanse of Llyn Conwy is spread before you: a great blue oasis in a desert of dusky heather and mosses.

Now gaining in confidence, the track descends north-eastwards to the shoreline, which it traces to a ladder stile in a tall cross-wall. Over the ladder climb left on the easier grasses which lie in the shade of the wall. At the top of the ridge, leave the wall side for another narrow path cutting east to the cairn on the western summit. The path continues across a heathery saddle to the east summit.

Descent

From the east summit, descend westwards to the path linking it with the cairned west summit, where a narrow path continues through the heather to meet a tall stone wall at its high point (GR 777470). Descend left by the wall before crossing a ladder stile near the shoreline of Llyn Conwy. Another narrow path through the heather flirts with the shoreline before veering slightly right to climb the

Opposite: Cwm Hafodyredwydd.

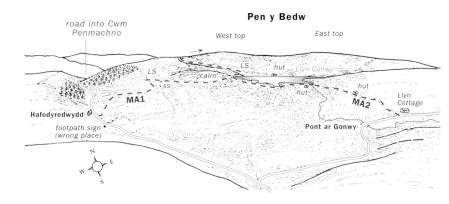

shoulder of the hillslopes to the west of the lake; note that the prominent cairn on this hill isn't on the route.

The path is faint in places but you should keep watch for a ladder stile in the cross-fence just to the left of a conifer plantation (GR 770461) – the narrow path you were on veers left just before this stile. After scaling the stile turn left on a grassy path running alongside the fence. Eventually you are confronted by a rushy hollow and some trees; there's also a step stile in the fence. Ignore the stile, turn right away from the fence, cross the hollow and follow its westbound course downhill on a raised grass bank, which makes the going easy.

The hollow becomes a rush-infested stream. As the stream changes course, veering to the right into Cwm Hafodyredwydd, it cuts itself a rocky gorge. Here the stream and track part company. The track, now lined with rushes, veers left down the now grassy hillside before reaching the road just higher than the cottage of Hafodyredwydd.

*Left: Climbing the slopes of Pen y Bedw.
Opposite: Llyn Cottage at the start of
Route MA2.*

Route MA2
Llyn Cottage and the Conwy Dam
A soggy walk around the lake

Start: Llyn Cottage (GR: SH 781446): space
   on roadside for a couple of cars only
Distance: 2½ miles/4km
Height gain: 460ft/140m
Time: 1½ hours

Llyn Cottage (Penty-llyn) lies near the summit of the Migneint road from Ffestiniog to Ysbyty Ifan. It's a gaunt stone building looking out across mile upon mile of sombre moorland and marsh. The Afon Conwy flows by and into the distance. That distance includes the sleek twin humps of Pen y Bedw, seemingly a long, long way away.

A stony track begins from the west side of the cottage. Pen y Bedw sinks under the skyline until the track comes to the dam on the southern shores of Llyn Conwy. The ground is very rough and Pen y Bedw still seems a long way off. A little angler's track sidles back left towards a stone-built outhouse and continues around the lake. Often the track is wet and covered with bright green sphagnum moss, so much so that you must surmise that the angler was wearing welly boots. The path becomes intermittent and sometimes it is easier to walk off it and on to the nearby heather. Make sure you follow the path to the left of the knoll (around spot height 460) or you might end up on the promontory and have to walk back.

The large cairn you see ahead isn't on the path but it signals the right of way (MA1) which joins in from the left. The route is now more ingrained in the heather and leads you to a ladder stile in a wall descending from the mountain to the lake. A forlorn stone-built boathouse lies just beyond the wall. Over the stile turn left to follow the wall to the brow of the hill, where a narrow path though heather leads to the cairn on the west summit. The path continues to the higher east summit.

Descent

The descent to the lake is straightforward (see MA1), but at the north-west corner of the lake the most prominent path climbs away right (this is MA1). Make sure you keep to the soggy but intermittent shoreline path, only leaving it for the short-cut avoiding that northern promontory. The stony path back to Llyn Cottage begins close to the dam.

Other route options

For those who want to make a day out of Pen y Bedw, there's a possible start at Cwm Penmachno. You could use any one of the footpaths from the lane south of Penmachno to gain the grassy spur of Lechwedd Oernant. There are helpful wheel-tracks to get you up most of the way to the east top. Alternatively you could use the prominent track from Carrog to the east of Cwm Penmachno village, climbing to the old quarry tips east of Moel Marchyria and the rocks of Y Frith Graig, where a public footpath leads east to the cottage of Hafodyredwydd and the start of MA1.

LINK ROUTE

Y Gamallt (Ffestiniog Mountains)

Distance: 5½ miles/9km
Height gain: 280ft/270m
Time: 2½–3 hours

This is a rough and soggy route, typically Migneint in fact. Basically use the MA1 route of descent along the ridge, down by the wall side to Llyn Conwy, along the little path through heather left of the big cairn and down to the road at Hafodyredwydd. You could make a direct ascent from here but it is better to turn left along the mountain lane, then right at the road junction. Leave the road using a stony angler's track on the right (GR 753430).

Beyond a small parking area the track becomes a damp but easily discernible path. The track eventually goes to the shores of Llynnau Gamallt's largest lake but leave it when you reach some rocky knolls. Turn right along the nearside of these knolls. A path does develop and climbs among heather and crag to the rim of the Graig Goch rocks. A pleasing path, with wonderful views across the Llynnau Gamallt lakes towards the Manod mountains, takes you to Y Gamallt's summit.

Opposite: Cwm Penmachno seen from the summit of Pen y Bedw.

As the Migneint's moorland shelf rarely drops below 1300ft/400m, its peaks don't impose themselves on their surroundings the way you'd expect them to. In this respect, Cerrig y Leirch, which lies at the north-western end of the range, is no different. But it is a splendid little peak, with crags and boulders enhancing its squat northern face, and while the Migneint has a reputation for being rough and boggy, this peak is friendly, with short springy grass carpeting the slopes between the crags. Were it not for the Afon Gam, which bars the way from this direction, it's the sort of place you'd visit for a summer picnic.

Cerrig y Leirch's outlying position means that it is one of the best starting points for an exploration of this great moorland desert, and it's easily accessed by way of the quarry on its western side. Once you've reached the summit you see what lies behind is a desert of grass, heather and mosses, relieved only by the oasis of pallid green provided by the valley of the Afon Serw and the huge hulk of Arenig Fach at the eastern end. There's a large lake, Llyn y Dywarchen, on the south side of Cerrig y Leirch and a smaller and more distant one, Llyn Serw, which is the source of the previously mentioned river.

The great feeling of spaciousness here is uplifting, as is the freedom to roam in any direction without either eroded paths or barbed wire fences to bar your way.

Left: Approaching Cerrig y Leirch from the quarry.
Right: Looking across the shoulder of Y Garnedd to Manod Mawr.

Route MA3
Llyn Dubach

A fine introduction to the Migneint
Start: Parking by Llyn Dubach,
　　Ffestiniog–Ysbyty road (GR: SH 746424)
Distance: 1 mile/1.5km
Height gain: 360ft/110m
Time: 30–40 minutes

From the car park entrance turn right along the road for a few paces, then left on a quarry track which fords a stream. Although the whole area is listed as an access area, there are areas fenced off and tracks with 'No Walkers' signs daubed on their entrances. The current litigious society has meant the authorities are worried about you diving into one of the quarry pits and suing them because you hurt yourself. To avoid these areas this route will keep to the left (north) side of the quarry.

Follow the slate track eastwards and across the Afon Gam and turn left at the first junction. This brings the route to an area where the quarry dressing sheds used to be (you'll see a flat concrete area on the right). Turn left along a track that runs alongside the river and follow this to the old weir.

Maintain direction across grassland out of the quarry with a fence at first on your right and the rocky ramparts of Cerrig y Leirch ahead. Beyond a fence corner, where the fence turns away right, head across rough grassland and rushes towards the right (southeast) side of the crags. By contouring around the huge outcrop on the right you will locate the simplest and the driest grassland to reach the unmarked summit.

Cerrig y Leirch

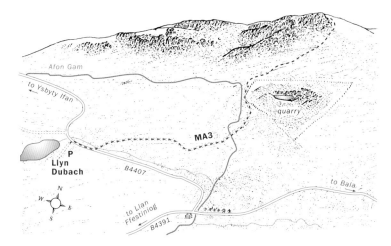

Above: Looking from Cerrig y Leirch across Llyn Dywarchen to Arenig Fach.

RIDGE ROUTE

Carnedd Iago
Distance: 2 miles/3.3km
Height gain: 150ft/45m
Time: 1 hour

Head SSE on the highest ground where you'll soon come across Llyn y Dywarchen. Pass to the west and the south of the lake. The crossing of the outflow is marshy and riven with rushes but quite passable. You'll see Carnedd Iago ahead beyond a moorland hollow and with forestry on its south-west flanks. Wheel-tracks help you to find a good course across the hollow and bring you to the fence corner just short of the forest's top edge. The fence will now lead all the way to Carnedd Iago's summit.

CARNEDD IAGO

Carnedd Iago, James's cairn, is a rather dull peak, robbed of its Migneint wildness by a forest of larch and spruce which spread from the old Ffestiniog road almost to its summit. Only an intersection of fences and an old boundary stone mark the summit, the high point in a vague ridge between Arenig Fach and the Ysbyty Ifan high road (the cairn must have been flattened years ago).

Carnedd Iago's saving grace is its easy access and its grand viewpoints, which stretch for miles when you turn your back to the forestry. Beneath your feet the ground declines gradually to the snaking Afon Serw, which on its short course to feed the Afon Conwy is as wild as any river in Wales. If Emily Brontë had been looking for another dramatic setting for Wuthering Heights, then Cefngarw would fit the bill. On a desolate moorland shelf overlooking the river, this rugged stone-built dwelling is so isolated I can almost imagine Heathcliff emerging from the rustic wooden front door.

Further afield, blue lakes are scattered across the plateau. Of these Llyn Conwy, the source of the great Conwy river, and Llyn Dywarchen are most prominent, while little Llyn Serw lies on high ground above Cefngarw.

All this drama makes the urge to venture into this wilderness irresistible and, although the bright colourful spots are probably bog, the walker will be rewarded with wonderful silence, unlimited space and beautiful air untainted by the excesses of the twenty-first century.

Opposite: Near the summit of Carnedd Iago looking to Arenig Fach.
Above: Looking across the Migneint to the Glyderau peaks from Carnedd Iago.

Route MA4
South Slopes

A first step on to the Migneint

Start: B4391 west of Llyn Celyn: roadside
    parking next to forest road entrance
    (GR: SH 787396)

Distance: ¼ mile/1.3km

Height gain: 280ft/85m

Time: ½ hour

There are two parallel routes from the start of the walk from the Llyn Celyn–Ffestiniog road. The forestry route (if there are no ongoing forestry operations it's easier underfoot) and the forest's eastern perimeter (which is rougher). Both meet at the perimeter fence (GR 782482).

The forest route simply follows the pleasant forest track to a junction where you'll see Carnedd Iago beyond a clearing. Turn right and follow a rough track for a short way to the gate on the perimeter. Through this follow the fence on the right, across rough moor to the summit, where there is an intersection of fences and an old border stone.

The moor route climbs north-west from the roadside, tracing the forest's edge. There's a slight drop where Nant yr Olchfa dissects the hillslope. Beyond this the route continues the climb by a fence on the left to the summit.

Other route options

You could start in the Conwy Valley south west of Ysbyty Ifan and follow the marked footpath from GR 814456 and follow it through the Serw Valley to the lonely shepherd's cottage at Cefngarw. Now you would have to ford the river (difficult if in spate) and climb SSW across rough moor to Carnedd Iago's summit. You'd have to have a strong resolve not to be enticed on to nearby Arenig Fach, which looks very impressive when seen from the banks of the Serw.

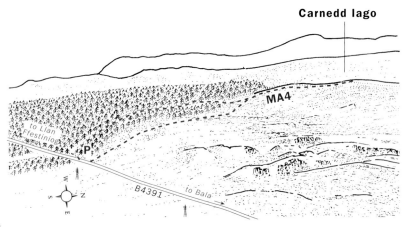

RIDGE ROUTES

Arenig Fach

Distance: 2½ miles/4km
Height gain: 975ft/295m
Time: 1¼ hours

Descend the squelchy moorland eastwards then north-eastwards by the fence to the marshy ground between the Afon Serw and Nant Gwyn. On reaching the low shoulder of Arenig Fach at Carnedd y Gors-gam, break away from the fence and climb the ever-steepening slopes of the main peak. Gradients eventually ease and you arrive at the summit cairn and trig point.

Cerrig y Leirch

Distance: 2 miles/3.3km
Height gain: 1310ft/ 40m
Time: 1 hour

Descend west alongside the fence and forest. Where the fence turns left you'll see faint wheel-tracks descending gently north-westwards but keeping to the high ground. Llyn y Dywarchen is a landmark which at first sinks beneath the skyline. The track shown in black dashes on the map bisecting the route at GR 770416 doesn't exist on the ground and it's not worth seeking out the marked border stones – they are neither attractive nor helpful to finding the easiest terrain.

The wheel-tracks curve westwards to the top of the next hill, which is greener than the rest because is has less heather. On the top of this you'll come across the expansive waters of Llyn y Dywarchen. Go round the lake on the south side – it's wet and rush-ridden in the surrounds of the outflow stream but passable. Cerrig y Leirch lies ahead although from this vantage point it's dominated by the crags of Y Garnedd, a peak on the far side of the Ysbyty Ifan high road. Again, keep to the high ground and you'll reach Cerrig y Leirch's craggy peak quite quickly.

Left: On the summit of Carnedd Iago looking across the Migneint towards the Moelwyn peaks.

Foel Fawr, the big bare hill, stands on the edge of the Migneint overlooking Trawsfynydd, its large lake and the concrete shell of its redundant nuclear power station. This hill is not big on features, a fact not lost on walkers who seldom come this way.

On the northern slopes there's an expansive cloak of green-black conifers, while to the east there's an ill-defined ridge stretching to the slightly higher Graig Wen. Foel Fawr is definitely worth visiting when the sun shines not too high in the sky, lighting the pallid moor grasses to a lovely shade of gold. At such a time Foel Fawr is playing at being part of a Van Gogh or Cézanne scene, with gem-like tarns and tiny pools hiding in folds of the ridges and shady hollows on the hillsides.

The summit panorama includes Snowdon, some of the Glyderau and Carneddau peaks, Cadair Idris and the Rhinogydd, but it is the nearby Moelwyn mountains which captivate with their ruggedness, the distinctive angular shapes of their crags and the Stwlan Dam, which grimaces from high on the mountain like a set of concrete teeth.

Nearer still, by a farmhouse on Foel Fawr's western side, lies the strange mound of Tomen-y-mur. This is the site of an early Norman motte-and-bailey castle which lies in the grounds of a Roman outpost, strategically sited on their military road between Caerhun in the Conwy Valley and Pennal on the Dyfi Estuary. The station included the usual barracks, a parade ground, bathhouse and an amphitheatre. Roman military practice camps are also evident at Dolddinas to the south of Foel Fawr.

Opposite: Approaching the summit of Foel Fawr.
Above: The approach to Llyn yr Oerfel with Foel Fawr ridge ahead.

Route MA5

Tomen-y-mur and Llyn yr Oerfel

A stimulating short walk with fine panoramas

Start: Tomen-y-mur car park above Trawsfynydd (GR: SH 708389)

Distance: 2 miles/3km

Height gain: 755ft/230m

Time: 1¼ hours

From the Tomen-y-mur car park turn right on to the road. Where this turns left go straight ahead along the clear quarry track heading east. It soon comes to the shores of Llyn yr Oerfel, beyond which the fields of Tir-y-mynydd farm make a perfect foreground for the pale moorland ridges of Foel Fawr.

About 100 yards/m past the farm, leave the quarry track for a rutted route veering slightly left up grassy hillside towards the ridge ahead. Below you on the right at this stage are the crumbling ruins of the old quarries then, a bit further on, the sheds and plant of an active quarry.

The path swings left as another lake comes into view. Now heading northwards it climbs beneath the main ridge before coming to the twin breached stone dams of two small reservoirs, which today contain little water. The path fades for a short while but continue northwards through a hollow with the marshiest ground to your right. The path soon resumes and takes the route level with Llyn Craig-y-tan, a tarn with a few small islands and a splendid view of the Moelwyn and Snowdon ranges.

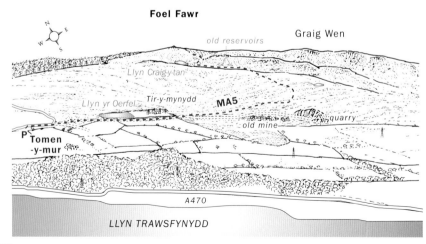

Now the paths on the ground do fade, but the grassy terrain makes progress easy. Turn right (eastwards) to climb by a rash of boulders to reach another small tarn. Now the rock-fringed summit of Foel Fawr is in full view ahead. Follow a crag-interspersed ridge to the right of the hollow to a point where it levels off, then climb left to the summit cairn.

Other route options

It is perfectly feasible to use forest tracks from the Roman road at Sychnant, which lies just to the north of the Route MA5 start point.

Below: On the summit of Foel Fawr looking to Moelwynion.

RIDGE ROUTE

Graig Wen

Distance: 1 mile/1.4km
Height gain: 280ft/85m
Time: 30–40 minutes

There's no path linking the two peaks but, although the ground is marshy around some of the small pools and tarns which are scattered across the moor, it is quite a pleasant journey. Keep to the high ground at first, using the forest as a guide to progress. Round Llyn y Graig Wen on the north side before climbing bouldery hollows between crags to reach the summit cairn.

GRAIG WEN

Graig Wen, which means white crag, is the highest summit in a group of craggy moors bounded by the A470, A4212 and B4391 west of Trawsfynydd. Lying at the western edge of the wild Migneint moors, it is a rambling sort of mountain, with no clear ridges, not a lot of shape and not enough crags to raise your pulse rate. However, it makes up for this by the sheer number of pools and small lakes, which reveal themselves one at a time as you walk among them on the vague undulating ridge between it and Foel Fawr.

The summit is topped with a modest cairn competing with a scattering of rocks and outcrops. Sheltering beneath its steep, bouldery western slopes is a large lake, Llyn y Graig Wen, but you'll have to wander to the western edge to see it. There's a breached stone-built causeway and dam at its southern end and you can still trace the old shorelines of what was once a larger lake.

Graig Wen's trump card is its mountainous backdrop. It is encircled by nearly all the big peaks of Snowdonia. Across the Vale of Ffestiniog the Moelwynion are looking at their best, especially if the late afternoon sun is playing hide and seek in their corries and

Opposite: The summit of Graig Wen looking to the Arenig peaks.

125

crags. Snowdon rises sedately behind, while the domes of the big and little Manod lead the eye to the heather and vast moor grass slopes of the wild Migneint. Move around to face the south and Arenig Fawr is boastful, with its twin peaks rising mightily from a vast plinth of moor, overshadowing the Aran, Rhobell and Cadair Idris peaks, which recede into the misty blue of the horizon.

Graig Wen and its satellites have history too, for the Romans were here. To the west you can see the hump of the Tomen-y-Mur fort, next to which is a Roman amphitheatre. Their road, Sarn Helen, cuts across the moorland, and the practice camps of Dolddinas lie to the south. Come here on a late afternoon in autumn and watch the straw-coloured grasses turn orange, the lakes glimmering blue to pink and the mystical aura of the place come to life. Exercising a little imagination, you can almost see the soldiers marching by.

Above: Looking from the summit of Graig Wen to Foel Fawr.

Route MA6
Hafod Fawr Forest

A moorland walk but with views

Start: Tomen-y-mur car park above Llyn
Trawsfynydd (GR: SH 708389)

Distance: 2 miles/3km

Height gain: 935ft/285m

Time: 1¼ hours

After turning right out of the car park on to the lane, it soon turns left, heading north past a TV mast. Just beyond a small conifer plantation, leave the lane turning half-right by a footpath signpost (GR 710397). The rutted grass track used here heads north-east towards a larger spruce plantation before veering right (eastwards). The now soggy track eventually enters the Hafod Fawr plantations, where it improves for a while into a firm stony track.

On leaving the forest continue on what is once again a grassy track. It now hugs the south side of the forest. Leave the track as it levels off at the foot of Graig Wen's north ridge. Climb the trackless ridge. As height is gained small lakes appear in moorland hollows, while craggy outcrops stud the ridge.

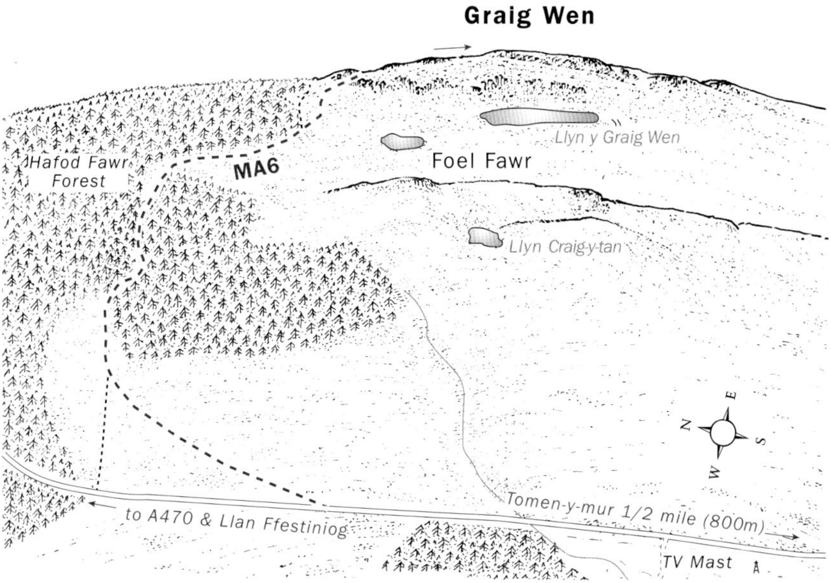

Graig Wen

127

Route MA7

Dolddinas and Llyn y Graig Wen

A pleasing walk with historical interest
Start: A4212 Cwm Prysor (GR: SH 728360)
Distance: 2¼ miles/4.5km
Height gain: 1080ft/330m
Time: 1¼ hours

Follow the lane northwards as it climbs to the farm at Bwlch-gwyn-uchaf, then continue on the unsurfaced lane beyond. This climbs along the perimeters of high pastureland on the left and stark moorland on the right. After climbing over the shoulder of the moor the lane descends and arcs right to the fields and Roman practice works of Dolddinas.

At the bend in the stony track (GR 733379) just to the west of the ruined farmstead here-abouts, head northwards on the right-hand one of three rutted tracks. You'll be able to see it climb the hillside as a swathe of green amid the pale moor. The track veers left halfway up to avoid a steep slope, swings north again for a while, then swings right along the slopes beneath Llyn y Graig Wen. The track ends by an overgrown water leat.

Follow this for a short way, then turn north-wards on another leat. Soon Llyn y Graig Wen comes into view as does its little breached dam. Cross the outflow by the dam before continuing the climb ENE on trackless crag-studded slopes – resist the urge to tackle the steeper stony slopes which rise from the lake. As you reach the shoulder of the moor, climb northwards to the small summit cairn.

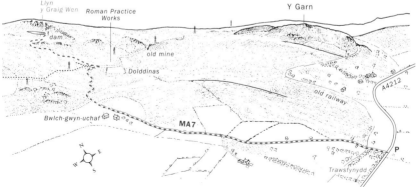

Graig Wen

Opposite: Climbing away from Hafod Fawr forest on to Graig Wen's north slopes.

Other route options

It is possible to start at Tomen-y-mur and follow the stony quarry track eastwards past Llyn yr Oerfel and its continuation to the shoulder of the moor at GR 720384. A faint track veers left before heading north-east beneath the steep grass slopes of Foel Fawr.

Ahead you'll soon see the track used in Route MA7 and you'll meet it near its end by the water leat. Now use MA7 to the summit. A longer route could follow the stony quarry track all the way from Tomen-y-mur to Dolddinas.

Note: from the ruins of Dolbelydr use the track marked with black dashes on the Explorer map and not the RUPP, which doesn't exist on the very rough ground it crosses. There is also a route using the old railway trackbed by the A4212 at Cwm Prysor and the bridleway passing Hiraethlyn and Dolddinas.

Below: Climbing Graig Wen from Dolddinas.

LINK ROUTES

Foel Fawr
Distance: 1 mile/1.4km
Height gain: 165ft/ 50m
Time: ½ hour

There are no paths along the ridge. Stick to the highest ground to avoid any marshy areas surrounding the ridge's tarns. Descend northwards from Graig Wen's summit cairn to avoid the steep stony west flanks. On nearing the edge of the forest descend left, keeping the first of many small lakes to the left. Foel Fawr's distinctive domed summit appears and disappears as you strike forward across the rolling moorland, never far away from the forest's edge. The mid regions are marshy but short-lived, and soon you're climbing the final slopes to the summit cairn.

Y Garn (Craig Aderyn)
Distance: 2½ miles/4km
Height gain: 260ft/ 80m
Time: 1½ hours

There are few paths on this trek but descend ESE on tussocky grass slopes. After around a mile/1.5km veer slightly right (south-east) to avoid the marshy terrain of two streams feeding the lakes of Conglog and the Llafar valley. You should reach a track at Bwlch y Llu beneath a line of electricity pylons at about GR 749385.

Follow the track for a short way eastwards but leave it at the apex of the second meander (GR 751386) and head south for a short distance to pick up a narrow shepherds' trod, which heads eastwards. This fades in marshy land on the approaches to Llyn Conglog-bach but a fence acts as a guide. Step across the fence by the lakeshore to avoid getting wet feet, then back to step over the intersecting north–south fence.

Head south now, following the fence's extension, a substantial drystone wall heading towards the heather knolls of Y Garn. The wall leads through a passage between hills to reach the huge lake of Llyn y Garn. It is low and easily crossable by the shoreline (GR 758378). After rounding the west shore, climb south to the little cairn on Y Garn's summit.

Y GARN (CRAIG ADERYN)

Y Garn may be small both in girth and in height, but it is rugged with precipitous rocky flanks, screes, heather and tussocky grass. To make matters more complicated it is protected by huge drystone walls which arc nearly all the way round its circumference and imprison its large heather-surrounded lake, Llyn y Garn. I spent as much of my time looking for breaches in this wall as on routes to the summit.

Much of the upper mountain consists of a mix of crag and heather with rides of tussocky grass bordering streams. These often, but not always, offer easier ways through the roughest terrain. The summit itself has the tiniest of cairns, unusual for a mountain whose name means the cairn. From it your eyes can meander around the sinuous shorelines of Llyn y Garn, whose sheer size comes as a surprise.

Y Garn's best feature is man-made, the old Great Western Railway line which linked Bala with Trawsfynydd and Blaenau Ffestiniog. The railway has been cut into the rock faces overlooking Cwm Prysor – a marvellous feat of Victorian engineering. The viaduct spanning the infant Afon Prysor has nine brick arches and is 105feet/32m above the river at its highest point. The railway closed in 1961.

On the south side of the mountain just below the railway is Castell Prysor, a Welsh medieval motte-and-bailey castle set on a natural rock outcrop. One of the few historical references to the castle is a letter sent from here in 1284 by Edward I.

Left: Looking back along the old railway used on Route MA9.
Above: Crossing the viaduct near the start of Route MA8.

Route MA8
Cwm Prysor and the old railway
A tough but stimulating moorland walk

Start: A4212 Llyn Tryweryn: junction
    with old Bala–Blaenau railway trackbed
    (GR: SH 784387)

Distance: 2½ miles/4km

Height gain: 560ft/170m

Time: 1¼ hours

The old trackbed, which shares its course with a forestry road, at first swings away from the busy A4212 road. Where the forestry track swings right and uphill through the conifers, go straight ahead on a grassy track, wet at times. This crosses a spectacular viaduct high above the farmhouse of Blaen-y-

cwm and the bustling infant Afon Prysor. The journey continues in spectacular fashion as the trackbed climbs to the precipitous craggy slopes of Y Garn. The distinctive craggy mountains of Arenig Fawr and Moel Llyfnant add interest in views to the south.

The mountain route proper starts by a metal farm gate on the right at GR 770378. Farmers' wheel-tracks set the uphill course with some old wooden telephone posts on the right. The tracks end by a ruined sheep-fold. Here aim NNW for a wall-end. The far side of the wall will lead you across ground made rough by heather and tussocky grass. Soon the huge Llyn y Garn appears in the view ahead. Keep to the north side of the lake and cross the crumbling wall at GR 758378

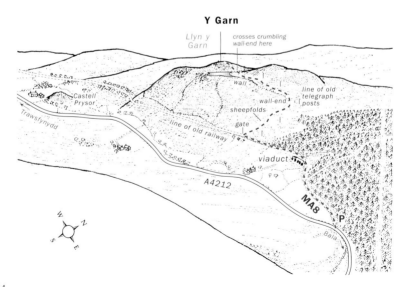

Above: The old railway track on a spectacular ledge above Cwm Prysor.

before rounding the west shore and climbing southwards to the little cairn on Y Garn's summit.

Descent

The key to the descent is to locate the wall leaving the north-western shores of the lake at GR 763378. If you follow this and some old wooden telegraph posts to the wall-end at GR 766381, then head SSE, keeping more of the telegraph posts to the left, you should find the sheepfold at GR 768380 and the track leading to the gate on the old railway trackbed.

Route MA9
The old railway's western approach
The easiest and most satisfying route
Start: Western junction of GWR trackbed
   and A4212 (GR: SH 728360)
Distance: 2½ miles/4km
Height gain: 800ft/245m
Time: 1½ hours

From the roadside lay-by on the A4212 cross the road with care and follow the lane opposite for a few paces before turning right on to the trackbed of the Great Western Railway's Bala–Blaenau Ffestiniog route. The grassy trackbed has many intervening gates and stiles as it swings away from the road towards the northern valley-slopes to cross the bridge spanning the Afon Llafar. A detour right is necessitated by the line being overgrown with trees.

Continue with the track past the great loop around the farms of Glasgoed and Bryncelynog. Just beyond a ladder stile overlooking the latter farm you'll notice an opening in a fence to the left (GR 754372). Once through this turn right, following faint wheeltracks up the hillside to a gap in a substantial drystone wall (GR 755372). Beyond this climb the heather bank, from where you'll see a grassy ride through the heather slopes ahead. This takes you nearly all the way to the summit. Where it divides, take the left fork climbing north-east before clambering up a heathery knoll to the little summit cairn, from where you see the massive Llyn y Garn for the first time.

Above: Castell Prysor.
Overleaf: On the summit of Y Garn looking across Llyn y Garn to the Arenig peaks.

Descent

From the cairn descend west down the initial heather knoll. Now aim to follow the grassy ride continuing south-west to a gap in a substantial stone wall (GR 755372). From here wheel-tracks descend rough pastures down towards a river and the old railway. Near the bottom go left through an opening in a fence. Through it turn right along the trackbed to the A4212.

Route MA10
Dolddinas and Llynnau Conglog

A longish route through fine moorland landscapes

Start: Western junction of GWR trackbed and A4212 (GR: SH 728360)

Distance: 4 miles/6.4km

Height gain: 950feet/290m

Time: 2½ hours

From the roadside lay-by on the A4212 cross the road before taking the narrow tarred lane opposite. Beyond the cottages of Bwlch-gwyn-uchaf, the lane becomes a pleasant unsurfaced track, giving views of Traws-fynydd's huge lake while gradually swinging right. It descends to the green fields of Dold-dinas, where the Roman soldiers had their

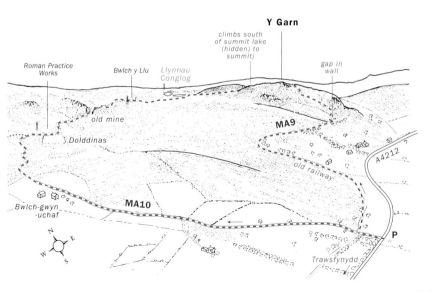

Above: Llyn Conglog-bach.

practice works. The earthworks still remain today. Beyond Dolddinas the track climbs towards a little nick in the straw-coloured hills ahead. Electricity pylons pass through the same nick, where you'll see the remains of old lead mines and a lively stream.

The ground gets more desolate as height is gained. At Bwlch y Llu the track passes under the pylons. It meanders across flattish ground north of Moel y Croesau. Leave the track at the apex of the second meander (GR 751386) to head south for a short distance to pick up a narrow shepherds' trod, which heads eastwards. This fades in marshy land on the approaches to Llyn Conglog-bach but a fence acts as a guide.

Intelligent navigation will avoid the worst of the marshland. Step across the fence by the lakeshore to avoid wet feet, then back to step over the intersecting N–S fence. Head south now, following the fence's extension, a substantial drystone wall heading towards the heather knolls of Y Garn. The wall leads through a passage between hills to reach the huge lake of Llyn y Garn. The wall is low and easily crossable by the shoreline (GR 758378). After rounding the west shore climb south to the little cairn on Y Garn's summit.

Other route options

A long approach could be made from the car park by Tomen-y-mur through to the Roman practice works at Dolddinas, where you could follow Route MA10 to the summit.

LINK ROUTE

Graig Wen

Distance: 2½ miles/4km
Height gain: 540ft/165m
Time: 1½ hours

There are no paths from the summit, but descend NNE to the wall at the north-west corner of Llyn y Garn (GR 758378). Follow the wall northwards to Llyn Conglog-bach.

Turn left by the south shore. You'll need to cross and re-cross a fence to keep dry feet.

A sheep trod materialises and takes the route west over drier ground on the north slopes of Moel y Croesau and takes you almost to the track marked on the map underneath a row of electricity pylons at Bwlch y Llu. Leave the path when you see this track. You should cross it approximately at the bend at GR 749385. Using the track would lose you too much height, so climb north on tussocky grasslands towards the skyline between Graig Wen and Foel Cynfal.

Once you're free of the marshiest ground surrounding the watercourses head WNW to reach the sparse rocks that are scattered on Graig Wen's summit area. The summit itself is marked by a cairn.

Below: Descending by the old mines to Dolddinas.

This fine little summit, which means the gorse crags, doesn't get much attention being well away from the major Snowdonian peaks. Sandwiched between the valleys of the Afon Prysor and Afon Gain, Craiglaseithin has a distinctive exaggerated dome shape with some impressive crags on its west face. A narrow marshy depression separates Craiglaseithin and the slightly higher Moel Oernant.

Lying in a deep complex hollow to the south of the summit is Llyn Gelli Gain, a splendid sheet of water with a small primitive dam on its south side. It's one of the surprises of eastern Snowdonia; and one of the great views when seen from the south-west. Heather and grass in equal measure, studded with crag, form a perfect foreground not only for Craiglaseithin, but for Arenig Fawr and Moel Llyfnant, whose distinctive outlines, crags and slopes are seen at unfamiliar angles.

The summit has a strange upright iron girder protruding from it. It is the base of a military flag-post, one of hundreds of relics from the time when this was a military artillery training area, established before the First World War but closed down in 1958 after the Ministry of Defence failed to get acceptance for their plans for an extended range. The old barracks used to be at Bronaber below, where the holiday chalets are now. You'll probably see the odd short stretch of stone wall on the way up, or a strangely positioned shelter. These were gun positions for the soldiers.

Opposite: Early stages of the climb to Craiglaseithin.
Above: A walker tackles the final slopes of Craiglaseithin.

Route MA11
Penystryd and Llyn Gelli Gain

A pleasant if unspectacular route
Start: Lane-side parking near Penystryd
  Chapel (GR: SH 726318)
Distance: 1¼ miles/2km
Height gain: 525ft/160m
Time: 1 hour

From the chapel, head north for the short way to the Trawsfynydd road and follow this to the signed footpath by Penystryd Farm. Follow the clear path for a short way. In the early stages the right of way follows the path marked on the OS Explorer maps with faint black dashes rather than the one in green. Where the path on the ground swings left back towards a wall and a tall white post, leave it and maintain direction on a faint intermittent path, which tucks between the moorland ridges of Moel Ddu (the black bare hill – it's actually quite pale from here) and Pig Idris (Arthur's Point).

The path veers north through a grassy hollow, passing to the right of a soldiers' shelter wall before coming to a low moorland col. From here there's a surprise view of Llyn Gelli Gain, a spectacularly sited tarn surrounded by knolls of heather and grass and punctuated by rocky outcrops and boulders. Behind it are the distinctive peaks of Arenig Fawr and Llyfnant, while to the left the attention is captured by the craggy dome of Craiglaseithin. The sheer scale and beauty of the place cannot be imagined just from looking at the map.

The onward route descends here to the west side of the lake's basin before climbing higher ground to the left. The final climb is steep but easy as short-cropped grass channels weave through the rocks of the southern arm.

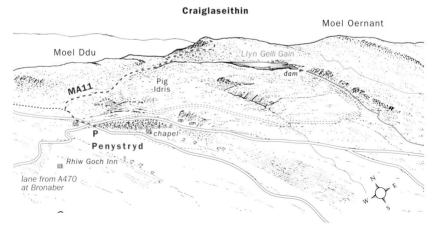

Craiglaseithin

Moel Oernant

Moel Ddu

Llyn Gelli Gain

dam

MA11

Pig Idris

chapel

P

Penystryd

Rhiw Goch Inn

lane from A470
at Bronaber

Above: Llyn Gelli Gain with Arenig Fawr in the background.

Other route options

It's possible to start at Trawsfynydd taking the minor road south of the Afon Prysor and the bridleway to Plas Capten. A right of way up pastureland to Ffridd Wen would make for a summit approach from the north.

RIDGE ROUTE

Moel Oernant

Distance: ¾ mile/1.2km
Height gain: 360ft/110m
Time: 30–40 minutes

From the summit make your way among the grass and rocks north-eastwards down to the broad moorland col. Moel Oernant is a massif bulk of a moor ahead with less rocks and more grass. The route up to it is still pathless and it is best just to maintain direction and climb the slopes, which are almost stepped, to the small summit cairn.

145

MOEL OERNANT

The name of Moel Oernant gives a clue to this hill's nature, for it means the bare hill of the cold or bleak stream. It's a bulky rounded hill, sparsely scattered with rock on the western slopes but otherwise covered with tussocky grass and rushes.

Drained by the Afon Gain, a tributary of the Mawddach and several streams flowing into the Afon Prysor, the hill has its marshy places. There's a small rather sombre lake, Hiraeth-lyn on the east side of the summit plateau, though how it gained the name of the lake of longing I don't know. A small cairn caps the summit as does a concrete flag base, a relic from the days when this was in the middle of an army firing range – you'll also see the crumbling remains of old military telephone boxes and telegraph posts scattered across the mountain.

Cow and sheep pastures stretch high on the northern Cwm Prysor slopes but the slopes of the Gain are typical Arenig: barren, treeless and eerily quiet. But in days gone by, the Romans were here. They had a practice works at Dolddinas to the north and their road, Sarn Helen, cut across the moors from Trawsfynydd to meet it. I've been unkind to this hill so far but it does have merits: the little stream of Nant Budr is lively, forming small waterfalls splashing over a rocky bed; the views of the Arenig, Moelwyn, Rhinog and Cadair Idris mountains are splendid, and you're near enough to Cardigan Bay to get the bracing effect of salty breezes.

Opposite: Moel Oernant seen across Cwm Prysor.
Above: The ridge route descending to the col between Foel Fawr and Moel Oernant.

Route MA12
Penystryd and Llyn Gelli Gain

A pleasant route on crag-crested lonely moorland

Start: Lane-side parking near Penystryd Chapel (GR: SH 726318)

Distance: 2 miles/3.2km

Height gain: 755ft/230m

Time: 1¼ hours

From the chapel, head north for the short way to the Trawsfynydd road. Go through the gate on the other side to follow a track bending right and raking south-eastwards up the hillside. The fine track enters the Gain valley with the river below and right.

The vast conifer plantation marked on current OS maps has been completely felled (2009), giving the hillscapes a wild and barren look. Hillslopes to the left are now gorse-scattered as the winding track arcs further left to come to the dam of Llyn Gelli Gain. Cross the outflow stream below the dam and follow a faint path which climbs boulder, grass and heather slopes to look across the expansive lake. The view is now dominated by Craiglaseithin, whose craggy dome lies at the end of a long bouldery ridge.

Head north on high ground to the east of the lake. Where the path gives out continue NNE towards the right shoulder of Craiglaseithin's ridge. This course will lead the route into the wide col beneath Moel Oernant. Again there's no path but once on the col you can pick an easy route north-eastwards over tufted grass and heather to reach the stone-built trig point of the summit.

Opposite: The lively Nant Budr seen on the climb out of Cwm Prysor.

Route MA13

Cwm Prysor and Nant Budr

A pleasant if unspectacular route

Start: A4212 east of Pont Dolydd Prysor
(GR: SH 749362), roadside parking just
west of the bridge

Distance: 2¼ miles/3.6km

Height gain: 820ft/250m

Time: 1¼ hours

From the small parking area just east of the bridge walk eastwards on the grass verges before turning right on a track opposite the farm. This soon bends right and passes an old stone-built outbuilding. The track becomes fainter here but a fence on the right acts as a guide as the path crosses fields. It makes a detour right before fording a side stream, then resumes by the fence to meet a cross-track by a copse of trees and sheepfolds.

Turn left through gates in the sheepfolds and follow the banks of a lively stream, Nant Budr, on the right. The rough stony track passes some waterfalls. In autumn the grasses surrounding the stream turn a glowing orange, adding colour to the scene.

Just before the track reaches its highpoint in a nick between the rounded Y Foel and the lower slopes of Moel Oernant (GR 750349), leave the track by going through two gates on the right. You'll see Moel Oernant now by looking half-right, but it's across the deep hollow of a stream so head south by the fence and wall on the left at first to avoid the marshy beginnings of infant streams. As you reach the high point of the fence climb southwest up grassy slopes.

This will bring you to the crest of the moorland spur, which will lead you to the north shore of a tiny lake, known as Hiraethlyn, the lake of longing (it is not named on current maps and should not be confused with a larger lake of the same name on the other side of Cwm Prysor). Now the route simply climbs westwards to the summit.

Moel Oernant

Descent

Descend west to the north shores of Hiraeth-lyn, then north-east down a moorland spur. Halfway down, as you approach the marshy hollow on the right, veer half-right to join the wall/fence, which leads downhill to the twin gates, allowing access to the track of descent. Turn left along this and just beyond some sheep pens turn right through a gate. Here a fence leads to another prominent track leading to the A4212 road.

Other route options

The lane-end (GR 755336) near the head of the Afon Gain offers a quick but pathless route via Hiraethlyn.

Above: On the track to Llyn Gelli Gain and Moel Oernant.

RIDGE ROUTES

Craiglaseithin

Distance: ¾ mile/1.2km
Height gain: 230feet/70m
Time: ½ hour

This pathless but obvious moorland route takes you south-westwards down to a broad grassy moorland col before climbing among grass and crag to Craiglaseithin's summit cairn.

Foel Boeth

Distance: 3½ miles/5.6km
Height gain: 1065ft/325m
Time: 1½–2 hours

This is a rather contrived ridge route but usable on a longer itinerary. Descend east passing the north shore of Hiraethlyn, then north-east for a while down a broad grassy spur, but on seeing a distant wall swing right (south-east) down the mountain's east flanks to join a stony track just north of the end of the tarred Gain valley lane.

Head northwards along the track, which eventually veers right past the ruins of Buarth-brwynog. About half a mile/800m beyond this take a right fork. The stream on your right divides. Ford the left of the two at GR 768349 (near the confluence) and follow the north banks of the right-hand stream towards the ridge. On reaching the ridge fence turn left to the summit of Foel Boeth.

MOEL Y SLATES

Viewed on the map, Moel y Slates looks as though it will be a peak worth visiting, being the most northerly top on the Foel Boeth ridge. Unfortunately it doesn't live up to its promise: it doesn't even feel like a summit, being only slightly higher than the surrounding land. An intersection of fences and a view across a wide marshy ridge to Moel Llyfnant are the only features, and few will give it a second thought on their way to that peak. The walk from the Prysor valley may look simple but in reality is a horrid trudge across wet, tussocky moorland and should be avoided.

Below: The rather drab summit of Moel y Slates looking through the gloom to Moel Llyfnant.

RIDGE ROUTES

Moel Llyfnant

Distance: 1¾ miles/2.8km
Height gain: 790feet/240m
Time: 1¼ hours

Descend on increasingly tussocky and marshy ground to the moorland col north of the spruce forest. The ascent continues along the northern perimeter of the forest before climbing by the fence up the vague ridge of Lechwedd Rhudd – there's a wire fence all the way to the summit crest of Moel Llyfnant.

Moel yr Wden

Distance: ⅔ mile/1km
Height gain: 105ft/32m
Time: ¼ hour

An easy route over grass and alongside the ridge fence all the way to the summit cairn.

Above: The summit of Moel yr Wden looking to Foel Boeth.

Moel yr Wden suffers from the indignity of the mapmakers having moved its name from the summit to the side of the hill to make way for the name of a pass, Bwlch y Bi. In the middle of the undistinguished Foel Boeth–Moel y Slates ridge, it is a pleasant if unspectacular place to be. Its summit is topped by a neat cairn, there are some upthrusting, steeply angled rock strata here, and it's nicely positioned for fine views to the rugged and more shapely Moel Llyfnant, which lies on the other side of the Lliw Valley. It's worth noting that the right of way off Moel yr Wden and along the Lliw Valley consists of much firmer and less tussocky ground than the ways off surrounding peaks.

Route MA14
Blaen Lliw

A wild walk to a remote, seldom-visited summit

Start: Pont Blaen-lliw (GR: SH 802336)
Distance: 2 miles/3.2km
Height gain: 590ft/180m
Time: 1–1½ hours

The path marked on the map starting to the east of the bridge, Pont Blaen-lliw, is unusable due to a lack of stiles over the initial walls and fences, but the stony track which runs from 200 yards/m north-east of the bridge has been used as a path. It heads up the wild valley of the Lliw, passing to the left of two ruined farmsteads. Leave the track at the second, Beudy Uchaf, and follow a faint track across rough ground to the left of its perimeter wall. The track continues to the east of the stream, heading roughly in the direction of a conifer forest ahead. Although the landscape is sombre it is enhanced by the shapely summit of Moel Llyfnant on the right.

Ignore the ladder stile near to the forest corner and instead continue up the valley, keeping to the left of the forest. The path is very faint by now. If you lose it aim for a sheepfold and then the easier, less tussocky ground that leads to the prominent stone-scattered grass hill of Moel yr Wden, marked Bwlch y Bi on current OS maps. The summit is recognised by its little cairn.

Other route options

There are contrived routes from Cwm Prysor using rights of way to reach the access area but there would be no point to them.

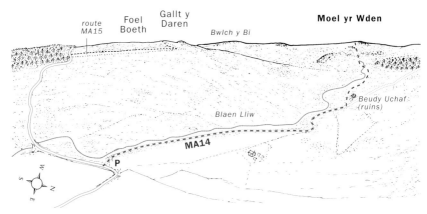

RIDGE ROUTES

Moel y Slates
Distance: ⅗ mile/1km
Height gain: 65ft/20m
Time: ¼ hour

A straightforward route over a grass ridge with a fence for a guide all the way.

Below: Moel yr Wden from Blaen LLiw.

Foel Boeth (Gallt y Daren)
Distance: 1 mile/1.6km
Height gain: 260ft/80m
Time: ½ hour

Follow the fence down to the col, Bwlch y Bi, then climb between the fence and a line of upthrusting rocks to reach the huge crag on the summit of Gallt y Daren. After a short descent to an intersection of fences turn half-left alongside the ridge fence to the second summit of Foel Boeth.

FOEL BOETH (GALLT Y DAREN)

Perhaps one of the least interesting 2000 foot peaks in Snowdonia, Foel Boeth is little more than a grassy hump in a long ridge to the west of Arenig Fawr. Overlooking the remote Lliw, Gain and Prysor valleys, Foel Boeth is surrounded by spruce plantations, although brief respite was gained in 2007 with the clear felling of the vast tract at the head of the Gain valley.

A high and remote country lane that links Llanuwchllyn and Trawsfynydd climbs to over 1740ft/530m above sea level, high on the shoulder of the mountain. It offers the peak bagger an easy and very quick method of ticking this one off their lists – it's just a walk by a fence on grassland. They'll find that there are two summits, one labelled on the map as Foel Boeth, the other Gallt y Daren.

Gallt y Daren has a nice rock outcrop for a summit. Like many of the surrounding peaks this area has been used by the army for training and Gallt y Daren has an old flag-post base and a rustic telegraph post nearby. Unfortunately, you'll look across the golden grasses of the Lliw Valley to Moel Llyfnant and the desire to be over there instead may prove irresistible.

Opposite: Foel Boeth seen across the upper LLiw Valley from Moel Llyfnant with the domed peak of Rhinog Fawr behind.
Above: The summit of Gallt y Daren, Foel Boeth.

Route MA15
Bronaber–Llanuwchllyn Road

A quick route with no problems or
*   excitement*

Start: Bronaber–Llanuwchllyn road
    (GR: SH 784334)

Distance: 1¼ miles/2km

Height gain: 360ft/110m

Time: 40 minutes

There's roadside parking by the forest road at GR 786322. Walk back up to the summit of the road and head northwards across the moorland ridge keeping the fence to the right. The ground is tussocky and marshy in places although it's never difficult, while the view across the Lliw Valley to Moel Llyfnant enhances the otherwise stark scene. The fence veers left on the approach to the summit.

Foel Boeth's south summit is marked only by a tiny cairn and the base of a military flag/telegraph post. The more interesting and higher summit known as Gallt y Daren lies to the north, and is clearly recognisable with an angular rock outcrop crowning the highest ground. There's just a shallow dip between the two.

Other route options

You could use route MA14 from Blaen Lliw to Bwlch y Bi then climb south alongside the ridge fence.

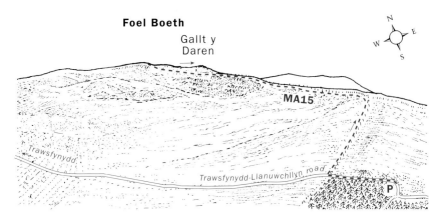

Above: On the ridge at Gallt y Daren heading north down to Bwlch y Bi.

RIDGE ROUTE

Moel yr Wden
Distance: 1 mile/1.6km
Height gain: 115ft/ 35m
Time: ½ hour

Descend northwards either on the rock-interspersed crest or by the ridge fence below and west of the crest. After reaching the pass of Bwlch y Bi, climb easy grass slopes to reach the cairn on Moel yr Wden's summit.

Above: Craig y Penmaen from the west.
Opposite: The old army observation post near Penystryd.

Craig y Penmaen, the crag of the stony hill, rises above the conifers of Coed y Brenin (the king's forest), the fast A470 highway and the Afon Gain. It's a distinctive and rugged little peak, coloured by heather in summer and with the fiery red of bracken for the rest of the year. The old Roman highway, Sarn Helen, traverses its high western flank offering easy ways to the summit from either the Coed y Brenin forestry plantations or the high country lanes linking Trawsfynydd and Bala.

Walkers starting from the latter will notice some strange buildings: firstly a concrete bus shelter-like construction, then a kiln with an entrance. They are in fact relics from the old military firing range, which dates back to the Second World War. The bus shelter was a sentry post and the kiln was an observatory. The soldiers' barracks were sited on the Bronaber holiday chalet site, while the officers' mess is now the Rhiw Goch pub.

Views from the top of this splendid little hill include a magnificent end-to-end panorama of the Rhinogydd range, which lies across the conifers of Coed y Brenin and the wild bare moorland expanses of Crawcwellt. Rhobell Fawr and Dduallt poke their heads above the spruce woods to the east, and the pale grassy moors above Trawsfynydd lead the eye to Arenig Fawr and Moel Llyfnant.

Route MA16
Penystryd and Sarn Helen

A splendid high-level route

Start: Lane-side parking near Penystryd
Chapel (GR: SH 726318)

Distance: 1¼ miles/2km

Height gain: 395ft/120m

Time: ¼ hour

Take the track leading SSW away from the road and the chapel. This passes a strange kiln-like building, an old army observation post. The track descends at first and is joined from the right by another track. Craig y Penmaen lies ahead at this point. Its northern crags are often in shadow, giving the hill a mysterious look.

The track levels out as it nears the crags and a wall that has been on the left for a short while veers left away from the track. Hereabouts you leave the old highway and cut across the grass halfway between the wall and the track to reach a wall intersection at the left-hand base of the crags.

A short scramble over boulders leads to a low point in the wall ahead. After stepping over it follow a wall on the left as it climbs steeply uphill. Take care not to snag yourself on some offensively placed barbed wire. As the ridge levels out climb right to reach the first of several cairns. The highest of the ridge's knolls is crowned by two close together and this spot is ideal for a picnic or a rest.

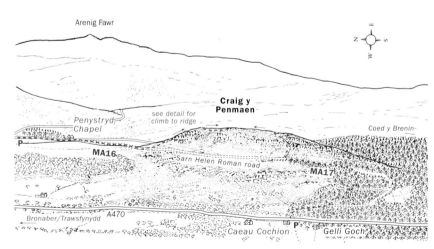

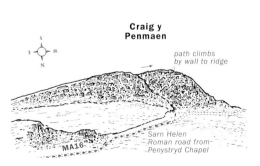

Craig y Penmaen

path climbs
by wall to ridge

Sarn Helen
Roman road from
Penystryd Chapel

MA16

*Above: The summit cairn of Craig
y Penmaen with the Rhinogydd on
the horizon.*

163

Route MA17

Bronaber and Coed y Brenin

*A woodland approach and rough trek
   through heather and bracken*

Start: Caeau Cochion Farm, 1½ miles/2.3km
   south of Bronaber A470 (GR: SH 715294)

Distance: 1½ miles/2.3km

Height gain: 755ft/230m

Time: 1 hour

From the lay-by cross the road on to a tarred unsigned lane which soon turns right passing through forestry. On reaching a signed footpath either side of the road turn left along the grassy upper path, which weaves and climbs through pines and larches to reach a forestry

road. Turn right along this, then left at the next junction.

The track, now part of the Roman road, Sarn Helen, climbs through more conifers to the open hillside, where heather, bracken and crag slopes swell to the skyline. This is Craig y Penmaen. At first there's a tall drystone wall stopping you from accessing the hill but soon, as the main track passes through a gate, another gate to the right (GR 722296) allows you on to open ground.

Although the terrain is rough, a path does develop and follows a wall on the right to the brow of the hill, where scrub, heather and bracken are replaced by moorland grasses and damp ground. The wall veers left to become the ridge wall. Where this levels out climb left to reach the summit cairn, the highest of several on the short ridge.

Other route options

There's an easy route from Ganllwyd following the Sarn Helen road, hereabouts a forestry track, as it heads north above the east bank of the Afon Eden. Leaving the old road at the gate on the right (GR 722296) allows access to the rough slopes used in Route MA17.

RIDGE ROUTES

None, although a link route to Craiglaseithin is possible. Just do Route MA16 in reverse by descending to the Sarn Helen track to Penystryd, then follow Route MA11 to the summit.

Opposite: Scrambling up the north-west slopes of Craig y Penmaen.
Above: Climbing the south-west slopes of Craig y Penmaen.

Rhobell-y-big, the pointed peak of the saddle, is a prominent pyramid of basalt rock protruding from the northern slopes of the much bigger Rhobell Fawr. Overlooking the lonely Cwm yr Allt-lwyd in the upper Mawddach valley, the peak issues a challenge to the walker who sees those crags towering above the heather slopes. There are no real paths among the final craggy diadem but grass and heather shelves and little rock bluffs make the clamber to the summit a joy to undertake.

Nearby a handful of streams have cut into the southern slopes revealing little rocky gorges hung with rowan and hawthorn bushes. The view south has been blocked out by the slopes of Rhobell Fawr, though the view in this direction is made interesting by the complex terrain of heather and rock knolls. Rhobell Ganol, the central saddle, promises a slightly loftier view but its crags lack the bold form of Rhobell-y-big. Views to the west and north are dominated by the Rhinogydd peaks, while the hollow of Cwm yr Allt-lwyd leads the eye uneasily over conifers to the rugged dome of Dduallt.

Opposite: Rhobell-y-big from Cwm yr Allt-lwyd.
Above: On the upper slopes of Rhobell-y-big.

Route MA18

Cwm yr Allt-lwyd

A short but wonderful climb

Start: Cwm yr Allt-lwyd road end
   (GR: SH 788292)

Distance: 1 mile/1.5km

Height gain: 655ft/200m

Time: ¼ hour

From the car parking spaces at the road-end, head east along the succeeding stony track for a few paces before leaving it for a track on the right, which zigzags up the grassy Rhobell slopes to end by the banks of an unnamed stream. A faint and narrow sheep-trod climbs half right (WSW) towards the banks of a parallel stream, whose craggy gorge is studded with rowan trees. Now the magnificent rocky cone of Rhobell-y-big appears on the skyline.

A shepherds' path continues not far from the banks to reach a ladder stile in a cross-fence. On the other side grass has been replaced by heather, moss and rushes. The stream, still on your right, is now shallow and its waters obscured by rushes. Just beyond a squat knoll of heather and crag it divides into two, making the rush beds easier to cross.

Head for some crumbling walls at the foot of Rhobell-y-big's crags – they are in fact the walls of an abandoned sheepfold. There are scores of ways up to the summit. Most are highlighted by angled grassy channels between the rocks. Crag rats will find plenty of short scrambles too.

Rhobell-y-big

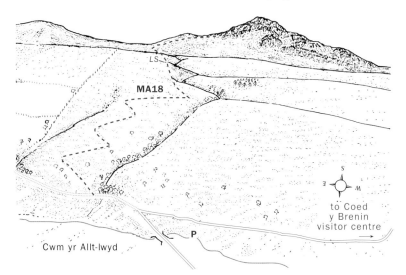

Cwm yr Allt-lwyd

to Coed
y Brenin
visitor centre

RIDGE ROUTE

Rhobell Fawr

Distance: 1¾ miles/2.8km
Height gain: 985ft/300m
Time: 1–1½ hours

There is little in the way of paths on this route. Clamber south down Rhobell-y-big's rocks to the tufty grass and heather plain below. Rhobell Ganol lies in your way towards Rhobell Fawr and, although it can be avoided on the left or right, provides an extra rocky summit.

After descending to a shallow marshy col continue with a steady climb on to the rocks and grass of Rhobell Fawr's vast northern slopes, known hereabouts as Llechwedd Llyfn. Route-finding is aided by a wall angling in from the west to an external wall corner. Follow the wall north all the way to the ladder stile giving access to the summit trig point on Rhobell Fawr.

Right: Scrambling up the summit rocks of Rhobell-y-big.

RHOBELL FAWR

Rhobell Fawr means the big saddle, an apt name for a twin-summited mountain of tremendous girth. Rising from the upper Mawddach and Wnion valleys north of Dolgellau, Rhobell Fawr's a bit too far off the beaten track to be popular, but for the connoisseur it offers great days out.

An old stony track not far from the church climbs out from the village and over the shoulder of Rhobell Fawr at Bwlch Goriwared before dropping into the coniferous plantations of Coed y Brenin. This was once a busy highway used by drovers but now offers walkers fine ways on to the hills.

Formed in great seas in the Ordovician period, Rhobell Fawr was an active volcano spewing molten ashes and lavas on the older Cambrian sediments. Although the distinctive cratered top of the volcano has long been eroded away, the crags you see today were all exuded from it. One thing you'll notice about Rhobell Fawr is that it has on the whole easy terrain, with much grass between the crags and little of the tangled heather and bracken seen on nearby hills. This is very welcome, considering there are few paths visible on the ground.

Sheltering from the north winds on Rhobell's southern flanks is the charming village of Llanfachreth, named after St Machreth, a fifth-century Irish missionary who lived in woods above the village – where the farm, Gellfachreth (Machreth's hiding place) stands now. It has been said that St Machreth was forced at one time to retreat to a cave on Rhobell Fawr, where he held services for his parishioners. The mountain was for hundreds of years known as 'the old church'.

Opposite: The summit cairn and trig point on Rhobell Fawr.
Above: Descending from the summit of Rhobell Fawr to the top stile of the eastern flanks.

Route MA19

Llanfachreth and Bwlch Goriwared

*Through high pastures with magnificent
views to a rocky climax*

Start: Llanfachreth – car park east of school
(GR: SH 756225)

Distance: 3½ miles/5.5km

Height gain: 1870ft/570m

Time: 2 hours

From the car park turn right to pass in front of the school then right again on a signed bridleway climbing through pleasant woodland and pasture. Maintain direction across a stony track serving the farmhouse on the left. The track then continues through the woods of Garth Fawr. Go through a gate on the right where it fades and continue on a path keeping the edge of the woods to the left. After heading north-west across the fields of Garth

Fach, the path meets a stony track which was once a drovers' highway. It heads northwards with the craggy mountainsides of Moel Cors-y-garnedd on the right and the western flanks of Rhobell Fawr ahead.

On reaching the col, Bwlch Goriwared, go over a ladder stile in the wall on the right and climb eastwards on easy grassy terrain. The wall on your right will guide you almost to the top. Faint pathways stay relatively close to it as they thread through rocky knolls. Avoid the temptation of keeping to the crest of those knolls as a steep descent down the other side will almost certainly follow.

Where the wall starts to curve around to the left as it nears the summit, leave it and climb left up a grassy rake between knolls. The summit cairns and trig point soon come into view ahead, and it's a short and simple climb to reach them.

Rhobell Fawr

Above: Nearing the summit of Rhobell Fawr from the east.

Route MA20
Llanfachreth and the south flank

A woodland approach and rough trek through heather and bracken

Start: Llanfachreth – car park east of school (GR: SH 756225)
Distance: 5¼ miles/8.3km
Height gain: 2000ft/610m
Time: 2½–3 hours

Turn left down the lane from the village car park. Ignore the lane coming in from Cors-y-garnedd on the left but instead continue on the wider lane you've been following, which swings right to another junction. The lane on the right, signed to Bont Newydd, has a fine stone arch, but it's the one on the left you want. This heads south-east through woodland and a forest, which at the time of writing was being clear-felled. Take the left fork through more forest at first then through high pastures with a stunning view across the wide

Wnion valley to the pallid rocky Aran ridges.

At another junction (GR 786218) take the left fork, signed as unsuitable for motor vehicles. This climbs more high pastureland. Its surface becomes more stony as height is gained, and soon continues through the spruce plantations marked as Ffridd y Castell (castle fields) on the map.

On reaching the upper perimeter of the plantation the now-gated track crosses a stream and turns right, with the craggy southern flanks of Rhobell Fawr soaring to the left. On reaching the third cross-wall at GR 788245, go through the gate but turn sharp left to climb by that wall up bouldery ground at first, then on grass and rock outcrops to reach the top wall running the length of the west ridge. Follow this right as it swings north. Go over a ladder stile beyond the turn – you'll see the trig point and cairns from this point – and continue south-westwards across easy grass to the summit.

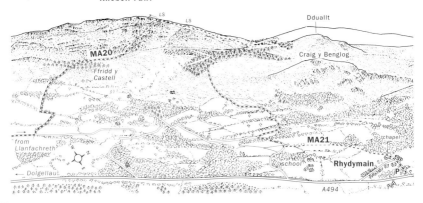

Rhobell Fawr

Route MA21

Rhydymain and the east flank

A woodland approach and rough trek
through heather and bracken

Start: Rhydymain – car park opposite village
hall (GR: SH 805221)

Distance: 3¾ miles/6.1km

Height gain: 1985ft/605m

Time: 2½ hours

From the car park turn left to follow the lane past the village hall and towards the village centre. Beyond a left-hand bend, take the first road to the right, then leave that for a track climbing left from behind the large chapel. This beautiful track rakes across wooded hill-slopes above the rooftops before reaching a high lane. Turn right along this, then right again at the next T-junction (there are spaces for a few cars here if you need to save half a mile).

The road climbs towards the southern edge of the large conifer forest filling the hollow between Rhobell Fawr and its neighbour Dduallt. Take the right fork at the road-end to enter the forest. After just over a mile, by which time the track will have reached the plantation's west perimeter, turn left to go through two adjacent gates by a stream which has come tumbling down from Rhobell Fawr's eastern slopes. Now follow the wall on your right to cross the stream. The wall finds the easiest way up the hillsides, avoiding some of the scrambles up rocks and boulder slopes to the left.

On approaching the first cross-wall veer left to locate the ladder stile. Once over this the way is pathless but you should be able to pick out the summit trig point on the horizon and soon the next ladder stile, slightly to its right, appears. After scaling this you're only a few paces from the top.

Other route options

There are a couple of possible routes from Cwm yr Allt-lwyd to the north, either by first climbing to Rhobell-y-big before tackling rough slopes over Rhobell Ganol, or by following the right of way south from Dol-cyn-afon over Foel Gron. Staying closer to the forest the ground is slightly easier.

Foel Offrwm is a tiddler of a peak ringed by the great mountains of Cadair Idris, the Rhinogydd, Rhobell Fawr and the Aran. But this craggy peaklet has a commanding position overlooking the Mawddach and the Wnion rivers. No wonder then that the hill has two forts, which are believed to date back to the fourth century BC.

Foel Offrwm means the bare hill of the offerings, and this place was used by the Druids for sacrifice, some say human, but besides Roman stories of ritual killings there is no evidence of this. The fort itself is ruinous but quite extensive. The views from it are stunning for a hill with such modest altitude. The lovely village of Llanfachreth can clearly be seen amid lush hillside pastures beneath Rhobell Fawr's serrated rocky top, while Y Garn of the Rhinogydd lies beyond the equally verdant Mawddach valley.

To the east are the grounds and mansion of the Nannau Estate. There's been a house at Nannau since the twelfth century, when the estate was owned by descendants of Cadwgan, Prince of Powys. That original building was burned down in 1404 after trouble between the owner, Hywell Sele, the 8th Lord of Nannau, and his cousin Owain Glyndwr. While hunting together on the estate Hywell, a fine bowman, swung round towards Owain and fired. Glyndwr was wearing armour under his tunic and the arrow bounced off him. After burning down the house Glyndwr killed him. The skeleton was found 40 years later in a hollowed-out tree but the house wasn't rebuilt until 1693.

Opposite: Fort on the summit of Foel Offrwm.
Above: Looking across the Nannau Estate and the Mawddach Estuary from the summit of Foel Offrwm.

Route MA22

From the Precipice Walk car park

A picturesque route to a fine hilltop fort

Start: Precipice Walk car park north of
  Dolgellau (GR: SH 746211)

Distance: ½ mile/830m

Height gain: 590ft/180m

Time: ½ hour

Cross the road out of the car park and rake left on a stony track and follow it to the first gate. Just through this climb the bank on the right to enter the access land of the hillside. Bracken is the main problem in finding a good way to the top hereabouts so head south on a channel through it towards a prominent tree, beyond which the climb proper begins.

You'll now be able to see a good grass track that rakes left up the hillside past thorn and rowan trees. It takes the route up to some low crags. Heather now replaces bracken. The track ends not far beyond the crags but there are trods through the heather and soon you find yourself at the summit fort.

Other route options

There's only one legal way to the access area: the way you came, but once there you're free to explore – maybe the second lower fort. Obstacles to easy progress are the heather and thick bracken, so it may be better to finish the day with a walk around the neighbouring Foel Faner using the Precipice Walk. It is a splendid, if over-popular, route.

Opposite: Looking from the summit fort of Foel Offrwm to Llanfachreth.

Foel Offrwm

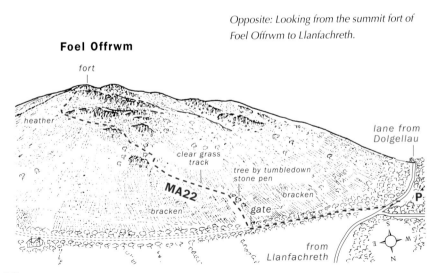

The highest of the Migneint hills is also an Arenig. Arenig Fach is for the most part a bit of a lump, with none of the best features of its big brother, Arenig Fawr. But the little Arenig has some secrets. Round the corner on the north-east side and away from roadside views, severe cliffs plunge into the waters of Llyn Arenig Fach. From here it's still rounded and still a bit of a lump, but it's a powerful lump with a sullen brooding aura. Arenig Fach has been body-building and looks well worth the effort of a foray.

Arenig Fach is seldom included in guide-books and when it is it has been unfairly described as a brute where only slogs through thick heather await those who undertake the climb. True, there are no real paths to the summit, but as long as you're fit this is nice. The bonus is there is no erosion, no orange peel and no Coke cans.

The easiest ways are from the south across low pastures to the heathery outlier of Y Foel. From here there's even a little path to follow through that heather. The summit is topped with a fine ancient cairn, Carnedd y Bachgen, cairn of the boy, hollowed out to form a shelter. It takes a detour eastwards to see the cliffs and lake.

For all the severe majesty of those cliffs and the dark cwm, maybe its Arenig Fach's connections with the Migneint that appeal the most. When you're standing on the summit looking across that vast undulating wilderness you cannot be anything but impressed, and when you're walking the Migneint, Arenig Fawr's western slopes seem to soar gracefully to the skyline. Surely it's not an Arenig peak at all; it should be Migneint Mawr or maybe Creigiau Bleiddiaid, which at present refers only to those northern crags.

Opposite: Looking down on Llyn Celyn from Y Foel.
Above: On the summit of Arenig Fach.

Route MA23
Bwlch Llestri and Y Foel

A splendid high-level route

Start: Fridd Bwlch Llestri, Tryweryn Valley
(GR: SH 817395)

Distance: 2 miles/3.2km

Height gain: 1150ft/350m

Time: 1½ hours

From the car park by the junction of the A4212 and the B4391 cross the B-road and climb to the gate on the far side. Go through this and the next. At the next fence-junction ignore the gate and turn right to climb northwards up the hillside keeping the fence well to your left. After passing under electricity pylons and skirting the left side of a rock and grass knoll the pathless route takes you through a rushy gap at GR 817400.

Cross to the right side of the gap for easier ground and head NNW for the left end of the tall wall in the distance. After rounding this climb over the next knoll and turn right keeping to the right of a marshy area. This is the roughest part of the walk but it's not too bad. You're now on heather.

Next climb eastwards up the heathery spur of Y Foel. At the top of this there are a few rocks and a good view across Llyn Celyn towards Bala. For the first time there's a little path and this makes a beeline for the summit cairn on Y Foel. The narrow path arcs through the heather before aiming north towards the heather massif of Arenig Fach. Where this path divides take the left fork which heads NNW up the slopes to reach a marshy plateau, across which Arenig Fach's summit comes into view. The narrow path cuts across the plateau but ends just before the boulders of the summit area. It's an easy climb from here to reach the summit cairn and shelter.

Below: The Route MA23 path from Y Foel to Arenig Fach.

Route MA24
Rhyd-y-fen and Craig Bleiddiaid

A permissive path gives the quickest access to the summit

Start: Fridd Bwlch Llestri, Tryweryn Valley (GR: SH 817395)

Distance: 1½ miles/2.4km

Height gain: 1150ft/350m

Time: 1¼ hours

The route starts opposite Rhyd-y-fen, where George Borrow stopped for ale after journeying over the Migneint. A signpost and stile opposite the junction of Rhyd-y-fen's drive and the A-road gives access to cow pastures. The permissive route climbs to the top gate, where you enter access land.

From this gate you can see the next objective, a gate in a tall cross-wall dividing grassland from the dusky heather moor. Beyond the second gate the route clambers up the steep heather slopes of Y Foel. After passing the rocks of a subsidiary top, a narrow path continues to the cairn on Y Foel's summit. Stay with this narrow path before taking the right fork, which meanders around the western slopes of Arenig Fach. By using this path you can get early views of Llyn Arenig Fach and the mountain's eastern crags.

After going across a stile in the fence at GR 825414 and in another at GR 824415 (fence not shown on current maps) you find yourself just above the crags and the lake. After exploring (carefully) the views head for the distant step stile in the fence on the left. Once across it you are on the rock and heather summit plateau with the summit cairn and shelter ahead.

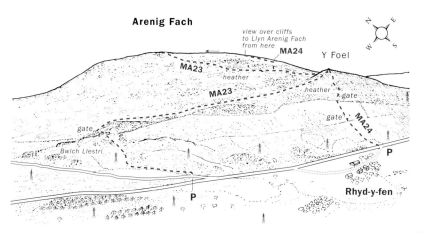

Other route options

There is an almost splendid route from/to the old kissing gate at GR 841402 (parking at Cae-garnedd car park and picnic site, Llyn Celyn at GR 845403). But it has two problems: where walls would have to be scaled at GR 843407 close to the farm buildings near Ffrith Uchaf where the path should enter access land, and just a short way further up the hill, where a wall cuts across the stream (GR 841408).

Beyond these obstructions a climb westwards leads the route past a couple of sheep pens on to a track climbing on to the south slopes of Bryn Du. After going through a gap in another wall cross a ladder stile and follow a fence-side path on heather towards Arenig Fach's summit. You'll join a narrow peaty path that has come from Y Foel. It weaves through heather and soon follows a fence above the crags overlooking Llyn Arenig Fach. Over another step stile the route heads north-west for the main summit.

It's also feasible to walk from Ysbyty Ifan using the old drovers' route to the sheepfolds at GR 841457 before following the fence on the right across the Marddwr stream. Follow this and the west bank of the Afon Gelyn before climbing south-westwards over Boncyn Crwn, keeping the Trinant stream to your left. Arenig Fach now overshadows everything and an intermittent path climbs the steep northern slopes and eventually reaches the summit shelter and trig point.

Above: Looking back down the western heather spur of Y Foel.

RIDGE ROUTES

Carnedd Iago

Distance: 2½ miles/4km
Height gain: 445ft/135m
Time: 1½ hours

Descend the heathery western slopes of Arenig Fach (pathless) then aim for the fence and border stones on the right. These lead across rough, sometimes marshy ground all the way to Carnedd Iago.

Above: Llyn Arenig Fach and Llyn Cleyn from the high slopes of Arenig Fach.

Carnedd y Filiast

Distance: 4½ miles/7.2km
Height gain: 1215ft/370m
Time: 2½ hours

Descend Arenig Fach's north slopes to join the Trinant (stream), which leads down to the wider Afon Gelyn. Cross with care, then turn left to trace the far bank to the cross-fence. Now follow this as it climbs right all the way to the summit of Carnedd Lechwedd-llyfn. Stay with the fence as it cuts across the head of Nant y Coed to reach the summit of Carnedd y Filiast.

CARNEDD Y FILIAST

Carnedd y Filiast, the hill of the greyhound bitch, the highest peak in the eastern Migneint, is a pleasant if rather undistinguished hill overlooking the upper Conwy Valley to the north. It's a heather hill with sparse crags but it's not without wilderness appeal especially when you look northwards across the immense moorland chasm of Gylchedd and eastwards across little Llyn Hesgyn, which lies in a sombre green cwm bound by an undulating ridge of minor tops.

If I have been dismissive of the peak, I still enjoy coming here for its quietude and its spacious views – you can see across the Migneint and the great craggy northern face of Arenig Fawr, while the barren neighbouring hills add to the sense of remoteness.

Carnedd y Filiast is one of three closely grouped summits separating the Conwy and Tryweryn valleys – the other two are Carnedd Lechwedd-llyfn to the west and Gylchedd to the north (631m spot height on the map). The high ground between them is tussocky and very much moorland in character, with heather, moss and tussocky grass covering soggy black peat.

Opposite: On the summit of Carnedd y Filiast looking to the Arenig.
Above: Ysbyty Ifan at the start of Route MA25.

To the south the terrain is drier, again with heather predominating, especially in the region of Foel-boeth. This makes a late summer trip a colourful affair. A shooters' track makes easy work of the mountain from this direction. The craggy little gorge of Nant y Coed is very attractive although the fording of the stream can be problematical after heavy rain or snowfalls. Other routes are provided by old drovers' routes from Ysbyty Ifan and Bala, which cut across the mountain at Bwlch Blaen-y-cwm and the east slopes of Lech-wedd-llyfn.

Route MA25
Ysbyty Ifan and Carnedd Llechwedd-llyfn

A drovers' route to the ridge

Start: Village car park, Ysbyty Ifan
   (GR: SH 843488)
Distance: 5 miles/8km
Height gain: 1755ft/535m
Time: 2½–3 hours

Ysbyty Ifan is well worth exploring either before or after the walk. The village was known as Dol Gynwal until the Knights of St John set up a hospice (ysbyty) on the grounds

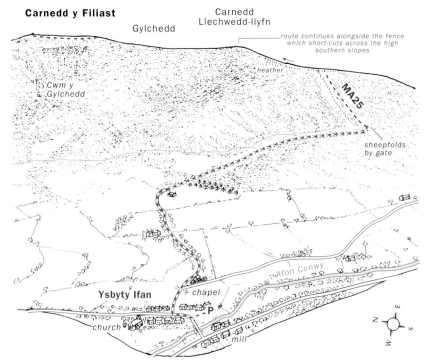

Above: The old drove road climbing south towards Carnedd y Filiast.

now occupied by St Ewan's church. The village was sited on a crossroads important to drovers taking cattle to the markets of England and pilgrims en route to Bardsey Island and Anglesey. You'll be using one of the drovers' roads on this route. There's a fine bridge spanning the Conwy, a well and a mill, recently refurbished by the National Trust.

The route begins on tarmac. Out of the village car park turn right, then right again. The lane divides on reaching the chapel and its adjoining cottages. Take the left fork here. The winding lane is now lined by hedgerow and climbs out of the Conwy Valley. Beyond the neat farmhouse of Ty'n-y-ffridd it becomes unsurfaced and passes through high fields and past a small copse of conifers. The land-

Above: Looking down on Llyn Celyn from near where the bridleway of Route MA25 reaches the ridge.

scape becomes increasingly wild with the huge rush-covered slopes of Gylchedd soaring from the equally desolate valley cut by Nant y Fuddai.

The track turns sharp left and ends by some stone-built sheepfolds and an old gate. The current OS map shows the old drovers' road continuing up the slopes ahead, but although you can see some wheel-tracks going roughly in the right direction they do not last. It is better to follow the fence on the left all the way to the ridge.

The ground, while rough for most of the way, isn't excessively so. For a short distance, at about the halfway stage of the climb, the route crosses the beginnings of the Sychnant stream, which, contrary to its name, is not that dry. The rushes help to keep the feet reasonably water-free before the route reaches terra firma.

On reaching the low top fence, which you need to straddle, make a detour to the top of the crag (505m spot height). Now you can see Llyn Celyn and the valley of the Dee, with Arenig Fawr on the horizon. Arenig Fach has been dominant for most of the way, but now you can see its dark tarn beneath its eastern cliffs.

Return to the fence and climb alongside it up the seemingly unrelenting slopes of Carnedd Llechwedd-llyfn, which has a shepherds' cairn a short way north of the highest point. The urge will be to continue to Carnedd y Filiast. The marshes at the head of Nant y Coed lie between the two tops and you can either keep to the highest ground on the left before tackling the final slopes to the trig point and shelter or you can take the direct route – with a bit of descent to the head of Nant y Coed – alongside the fence.

Route MA26
Llyn Celyn

A splendid high-level route

Start: Lay-by car park, Llyn Celyn
   (GR: SH 858410)
Distance: 3½ miles/5.7km
Height gain: 1540ft/470m
Time: 2 hours

From the car park by the shores of Llyn Celyn turn right down the road for a couple of hundred yards, then double back left on a rough forestry track that angles up the hillside. Just beyond a turning circle take the signed right fork track, which soon leads out of the forest and on to the open heath. Here it arcs right to

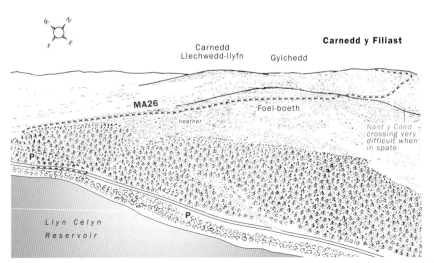

191

Above: Cwm Hesgyn with its little tarn.

climb beneath the crag fringed heather summit of Foel-boeth before dividing as it looks across Cwm Hesgyn.

Take the left fork, which heads north-east before nicking around the little gorge formed by Nant-y-coed. The stream can be very hard to cross when in spate and you may have to divert upstream to do so. After staying on the east side of the mountain the track suddenly swings left to climb to the summit shelter and trig point.

Other route options

There are several tracks from Llyn Celyn up Cwm Hesgyn, which would lead either to Foel-boeth or Llyn Hesgyn. The lake can also be accessed by path and track from the minor road at Cadair Benllyn to the east. Back at Llyn Celyn, there's also an old traders' route starting from opposite the Tryweryn Memorial Chapel car park to Carnedd Llechwedd-llyfn's west ridge, where Route MA25 leads to the summit.

LINK ROUTE

Arenig Fach

Distance: 4½ miles/7.2km
Height gain: 1310ft/ 400m
Time: 2½ hours

You could stay with the highest ground, heading north-west to Gylchedd (631m spot height) before turning south-west for Carnedd Llechwedd-llyfn, but most walkers follow the fence across the head of Nant y Coed to reach the aforementioned peak. It's very rough tussocky ground but a quicker and easier choice in mist.

Still by the fence, the route descends heather slopes down to the banks of the Afon Gelyn, a difficult river to cross. Cross where you feel safe but one of the better places lies at its confluence with the Trinant. Now climb by the north bank of the Trinant. Where the stream divides trace the left of the two streams before tackling the steep north slopes of Arenig Fach on an intermittent path, which eventually leads you to the summit trig point.

Above: Nant y Coed.
Overleaf: Looking north from the track on Foel-boeth, Carnedd y Filiast.

ARENIG FAWR

George Borrow wrote: 'Arenig is certainly barren enough, for there is neither tree nor shrub upon it, but there is something majestic in its huge bulk. Of all the hills which I saw in Wales none made a greater impression upon me.' Certainly, I know of no other mountain that seems visible from so many peaks as the big Arenig, whose twin peaks are so recognisable from any direction. This is because at over 2800feet/850m, the mountain is by far the highest peak between Snowdon and the Aran and everything to the east and west.

Arenig Fawr is a strange mix of mountain and moorland. Like Snowdon it's volcanic, part of Snowdonia's great ring of fire, and has a powerful angular mountain shape with great ridges and fine corries. And yet it forms part of a vast, inhospitable wilderness stretching from the modern Llyn Celyn highway to the Bala–Dolgellau road.

The eastern flanks and the summit of the mountain consist of thick beds of volcanic ash, while the crags of Daear Fawr above the northern quarries are of columnar formations of crystalline igneous rock. Llyn Arenig Fawr,

which lies in a deep cwm on the east side, has been dammed to form a large round reservoir supplying Bala and the surrounding villages with water. You'd think reaching the top of the cwm would bring you to the summit but this is not so, for this is a complex ridge and the rock is left behind for a grassy north-east spur.

The summit has a trig point and a large memorial to the eight crewmen of a US Air Force B-17 Flying Fortress, which in 1943 crashed into the mountain just below the mist-enshrouded summit. It has also been said that Welsh painter James Innes, who had been renting a cottage with fellow Welsh painter Augustus John at Nant Ddu, buried some love letters on this summit, his favourite mountain.

At the foot of the mountain are the remains of the old Bala–Ffestiniog railway track and Arenig station, which were closed following the Beeching cuts of the 1960s. This period was one of turmoil for the area, for about the same time Liverpool Corporation acquired permission to flood the Tryweryn valley for a new reservoir to supply the ever-growing needs of the city. The village of Capel Celyn, its school, post office, chapel and cemetery were as a result submerged beneath the rising waters of the new lake, Llyn Celyn.

Opposite: Arenig Fawr's east face.

Route MA27
Pont Rhyd-y-fen and Craig yr Hyrddod

A pleasant if tough climb

Start: Pont Rhyd-y-fen: park at junction of
    A4212 and B4391 (GR: SH 816395)
Distance: 3 miles/4.8.km
Height gain: 1705ft/520m
Time: 2 hours

From the park cross the busy A-road on to the narrow lane descending to Pont Rhyd-y-fen, with the great crags and quarry of Daear Fawr casting shadows across the views ahead. A short way beyond the bridge turn right on to a stony track, which parallels the old railway trackbed for a while before climbing left past an old quarry.

The key to the route here is in identifying a ladder stile in a substantial cross-wall (GR 815381). It's best recognised by the fact that by the stile the track becomes marshy and tangled with rushes. You'll see ruins in the mid-distance and a tree marking the site of Amnodd-wen and an old stone-built shepherds' hut on the left at the foot of the north-west ridge.

Just before this ladder stile turn left off the track for a faint track, which initially is wet and overgrown with rushes. Where the track just fades out veer right and climb alongside the wall on the right, aiming for the rocky summit of Craig y Hyrddod. The path soon becomes drier and more bold. The wall twists and turns as it negotiates the steps in the ridge and the increasing number of crags. Halfway up, the route goes through a gap in the now tumbledown cross-wall.

A new fence, under construction at the time of writing in 2010, now leads the steepening path up the rocks and on to Hyrddod's summit before veering off left. With only the scantest remains of the old ridge wall now visible, you turn right along the boulder-scattered ridge before climbing the last little rocky pyramid to the trig point, cairn and memorial plaque on Arenig Fawr's summit.

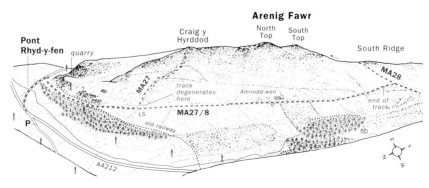

Right: The summit trig point and memorial to the airmen killed on the mountain during World War II.
Below: Approaching the north-west ridge.

Descent

Descend the rocky ridge north-east, then northwards to a fence corner (GR 829373) at the top of the north-west ridge before following the fence left. The ground steepens as the shaly path descends between crags but things soon ease and the ridge becomes grassy. Halfway down the path switches to the right side of a drystone wall, which leads the route down to the Amnodd-wen farm track. Turn right along this, following it all the way down to the old Arenig Road.

Below: On the track above Amnodd-wen. Overleaf: Looking from the north to the south peak of Arenig Fawr.

Route MA28

Amnodd-wen and the south ridge

A longish but pleasant route often used in descent

Start: Pont Rhyd-y-fen: park at junction of A4212 and B4391 (GR: SH 816395)

Distance: 4½ miles/7.2m

Height gain: 1870ft/570m

Time: 2½ hours

As in Route MA27, cross the A-road on to the narrow lane descending to Pont Rhyd-y-fen. A short way beyond the bridge turn right on to a stony track, which parallels the old railway trackbed for a while before climbing left past an old quarry. The track degenerates into a rush-filled hollow beyond a ladder stile lying at the foot of Arenig Fawr's north-west ridge. The driest ground lies on the left, well away from the 'pathside' wall.

ARENIG FAWR **MA27, MA28, MA29**

Things improve on the approach to Amnodd-wen, once a substantial farmhouse but now in ruins. Beyond the farmhouse the track becomes a beautiful grass path raking across the west flanks of Arenig Fawr. It terminates at the pass between the Arenig and Moel Llyfnant. A faint path maintains direction to meet a narrow path that has cut across the pass. Climb left with this path up the grassy sides of the south ridge. It meets a fence on the rim of the ridge and a primitive stile allows further progress.

The narrow path veers left to pass some shallow tarns, then climbs on a steep course to Arenig Fawr's south top before continuing by the ridge fence to the main north top.

Descent

Head south by the ridge fence, over the south top and down the south ridge. Keep to the narrow path on the right side of the ridge, passing a couple of shallow tarns before curving right to a primitive stile in a wire fence (GR 824355). Over this a narrow path descends grass slopes towards the broad col between Arenig Fawr and Moel Llyfnant.

Just before reaching the col a faint path angles right to the start of a fine grassy vehicle track, which leads down the valley to the roadside near the start of the walk.

Note: for a short stretch beyond the ruins of Amnodd-wen the track gets lost in a rush-filled morass and you'll need to step off it on the mountainside to the right.

Route MA29
Llyn Arenig Fawr

The classic route with a glacial tarn-filled cwm and many crags

Start: Arenig Road – roadside car parking area on the old station grounds (GR: SH 830393)

Distance: 3¼ miles/6km

Height gain: 1900ft/580m

Time: 2½ hours

From the car park turn left up the lane. Watch out for a track leaving the road on the right at GR 846395, about a mile away. Recognised by a ladder stile and a gate, the stony track climbs the western slopes of Moel y Garth. Soon Llyn Arenig Fawr comes into view in its great grassy hollow tucked beneath impressive cliffs, which are interspersed with heather and a little scree, giving them a sullen disposition.

The track ends at Llyn Arenig Fawr's dam and sluice gate. Cross its outflow stream – which can be difficult after snow melt and periods of rain, when many walkers brave an iron ladder conveniently placed across the water. Continue past the stone-built bothy on a narrow path that climbs the spur of Y Castell, the castle, presumably because of the rock-face on its northern flank.

From the top of the spur the scene changes with the cliffs being left behind. What lies ahead is a mountainscape of grass and boulders, with Arenig Fawr's summit massif appearing on the left. Accordingly the path swings left, traversing its high eastern slopes.

The path fades before the final objective and there's one final push over rock and grass to the summit.

Descent

The key to the descent is finding the start of the path, which doesn't quite reach the summit. Just follow the bouldery ridge to a fence corner at GR 829373, turn right alongside the fence towards Bwlch Blaen-y-nant. Where the fence angles slightly left (GR 830373) angle right across gentle slopes, where you'll meet the path as it traverses grass slopes below the east side of the ridge. Be careful not to walk too far north towards the cliffs above Llyn Arenig Fawr. The path leads down to the track by the dam of the lake.

Route MA30
Maestron and Y Castell

A solitary approach

Start: Parking off lane junction, Maestron (GR: SH 861359)

Distance: 3¼ miles/5.2km

Height gain: 1840ft/560m

Time: 2 hours

Turn right up the farm road with the Nant-hir stream babbling away to your right. The track climbs to the right of Cefn-y-maes farm. Where the track turns left for the farmhouse leave it for a grass track going straight ahead. Go across a footbridge spanning Nant-hir and head north to the next fence. Once over this head north-westwards across moorland

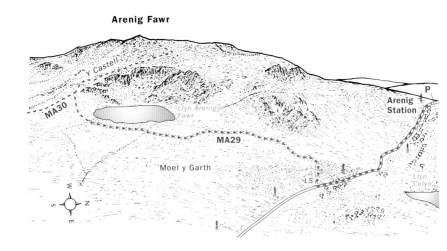

Arenig Fawr

Y Castell

MA30

Llyn Arenig Fawr

MA29

Moel y Garth

Arenig Station

P

LS

Llyn Celyn

of grass and rushes. The Arenig ridge spans the horizon across sombre moorland, but it somehow seems a long way off. On approaching the spur of Y Castell, keep to the right of the crag face of Carreg y Lefain.

You'll locate the main path up the spur just on its northern rim. Now moorland has transformed into mountain, with the glacial corrie of Llyn Arenig Fawr being flanked by sultry cliffs and dark heather.

Follow the path to the top of the spur, where Arenig Fawr's twin summits re-appear on the left. The path swings left, traversing its high eastern slopes below the ridge. The path fades before the final objective and there's one final push over rock and grass to the summit.

Route MA31
Maestron and Foel Blaen-y-cwm

See the Arenig mountains at their wildest

Start: Parking places at lane junction,
  Maestron (GR: SH 861359)

Distance: 3 miles/4.8km

Height gain: 1800ft/550m

Time: 2–2½ hours

Take the left fork but leave the lane at a left-hand bend to traverse a rough field on a faint track heading towards a ladder stile by a group of conifers. Trace the right-hand edge of the forest on a concessionary path (the much rougher ROW lies the other side of the small plantation). Ladder stiles mark the exits of each field along the way and a Landrover track soon develops.

205

Above: Climbing on Y Castell above Llyn Arenig Fawr.

Beyond the ladder stile and gate at GR 851363 the track divides. Take the left fork, raking south-westwards up grassy slopes towards the hillside's rocky fringe. The track doubles back right before reaching Foel Blaen-y-Cwm. Here it climbs westwards with the crags and twin summits of Arenig Fawr towering above a complex of craggy moorland knolls. The landscape is wonderfully wild and spacious, and the walking is easy – mostly the wheel-tracks wind over grass and heather. To the right of the route there's a wire fence, which would be very useful in mist because it stays fairly close to the route for most of the way.

After just over a quarter of a mile at GR 837365, the track becomes indistinct and a narrow sheep-trod climbs to a gate and stile in the fence. Go through this and continue on sheep tracks along the left side of a craggy knoll. This leads to a second gate, beyond which the route descends slightly to the hollow of the stream Y Merddwr.

The final extremely steep slopes of Arenig Fawr tower above you but there is a way up, following a grass and boulder rake angling left behind the shapely outlier of Carreg y Diocyn, to reach a col beneath the main ridge. There is craggy ground to the right so aim south-west for the saddle between the peak on your right (Arenig Fawr's south peak) and the 712m spot height knoll on the south ridge. This means there is a small descent before climbing easy grass slopes to the ridge. Once here turn right and follow the fence over the south top, then to the main summit.

Descent

Follow the ridge southwards, over the south top and down to the saddle north of the 712m knoll. Now look back left to a rugged col between the scree-strewn east slopes of the south peak and a squat rounded peak, Carreg y Diocyn. There's a slight descent before climbing to this grassy saddle. Now you descend a rugged hollow with the Arenig crags soaring to the skyline on the left.

Once at the bottom of the hollow, veer right and cross the stream. Keep a watch for a gate in a fence on the low ridge on your left (north). Climb to this gate and go through it. A little sheep trod wends its way east through crags on the south side of this ridge before re-crossing the fence. The sheep-trod soon becomes a clear path, then a faint but discernible vehicle track, which never strays very far from a wire fence on the left. On reaching Foel Blaen-y-Cwm it veers right before swinging left down to a ladder stile near a wall and fence corner (GR 848363).

Continue with the track as it traverses rough pastureland. Ladder stiles at field boundaries make the route obvious and the path heads for a narrow copse of conifers. Although the map shows the right of way going along the right side of the plantation, a concessionary route traces the left side before coming to the road at GR 859359 just short of the parking places.

Route MA32
Maestron and Dolydd Bychain

A fascinating seldom-trod route

Start: parking places at lane junction,
    Maestron (GR: SH 861359)

Distance: 4 miles/6.5km

Height gain: 1970ft/600m

Time: 2½ hours

Take the left fork lane heading beneath the mountainside but high above the pastures of the Afon Llafar valley. After passing Blaen-y-cwm-isaf farm the lane continues to Blaen-y-cwm-uchaf. Go through a gate to the left of the house, then follow the top wall across what can be a marshy field.

Go over a stile on the right into the woods of Maen Ymenyn, then turn left down to a footbridge over the bounding river (Afon Llafar). Above you are some very nice waterfalls. Over another ladder stile the path comes to some old sheepfolds and the ruins of an old smallholding. Ignore the stile on the left – it marks the start of another path – but climb past an open country sign.

Above a drystone wall a track leads uphill, heading SSW at first before winding past Craigiau Maesmatthew. The track soon fades and you need to get close to the Dolydd Bychain stream. Cross to the north bank – there are a couple of fences to scale – near the stream confluences north-east of Moel Ymenyn and resume an easier course on firm grass rather than the tussocks that would have greeted you on the south side. Sheep-tracks continue west up the cwm. The ground steepens as the narrow paths climbs into a mini-gorge heading towards the ridge.

Note: Above this steep climb a wide track develops. This is not the path wanted as it takes a lower course around to the west side of the south ridge. If you do find yourself along it you'll have to scale the southern end of the ridge.

The spur on the right becomes increasingly craggy and the path soon reaches a faint path to the right of the fence-line. This takes the route on to the southern end of Arenig Fawr's south ridge. Climb right here past several small tarns, then over the two summits of the Arenig Fawr.

Below: Dolydd Bychain stream seen from the footbridge.

Route MA33
Pont Blaen-lliw and the south ridge
*A wilderness approach with few paths but
    great appeal*
Start: Pont Blaen-Lliw (GR: SH 801335)
Distance: 3 miles/4.9km
Height gain: 1640ft/500m
Time: 2 hours

From the bridge over the Afon Lliw climb
eastwards along the narrow lane to its junction with the drive of Hendre Blaen-lliw.
Follow the drive towards the farmyard before
taking the right fork track that keeps the
house to the left before swinging right. Ignore
the left fork track and stay with the rough
track heading east towards the moorland with

the slopes of Moel Llyfnant rearing up to the
left. The track fades.

Beyond this you're left to your own
devices. The green dots on the OS Explorer
map don't help much, and what appear to be
paths on the ground are really the lines of old
drainage ditches when you get close. Ladder
stiles do exist in the fences, however, and
these will help you in the early stages. When
you pass under Moel Llyfnant's north slopes,
veer left away from the tussocky valley floor
to the higher firmer ground skirting that
mountain.

Once there, contour around to the moorland col between Moel Llyfnant and Arenig
Fawr's south ridge. Here you'll see the welcome sight of a path crossing the col. Ignore

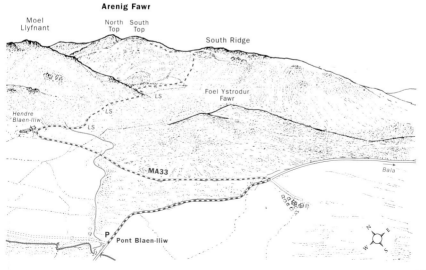

the left fork at the far end but climb directly up the grass slopes ahead, then alongside an old wall angling left to reach a primitive stile in a high cross-fence. A narrow path veers northwards to pass a couple of the south ridge's delightful shallow pools and rocky bluffs.

Beyond them Arenig Fawr's south top rears up. Follow the ridge fence up to its summit rocks. Looking back you'll see that the attractive south ridge is scattered with several pools and small lakes. Continue the journey northwards to the higher north top.

Descent

It's a straightforward walk by the ridge fence to the south ridge. From here the key to the route is to find the path down to the col between Arenig Fawr and Moel Llyfnant. If you go too early you'll have a needlessly rough and increased descent. The ridge fence soon leaves you to descend right.

Keep to high ground on the west side of the ridge, then follow a faint track that arcs right to a primitive stile at GR 824355. Over this path ease down grass slopes to the damp, mossy col between Arenig Fawr and Moel Llyfnant. Cross the col and skirt left around Moel Llyfnant, keeping high enough to stay on firm grass rather than the tussocks of the valley floor.

Opposite: The dry way around Moel Llyfnant to Arenig Fawr's South Ridge.

When you've passed the bulk of Moel Llyfnant head south-west across rough marshy ground to locate the ladder stile in the fence at GR 808341. Just beyond this you'll join the track leading to Hendre Blaen-lliw. Turn left on reaching the farmhouse. The driveway you're on leads back to the road a short way east of Pont Blaen-Lliw.

Other route options

There are numerous options from the track running along the valley of the Afon Amnodd-bwll. One begins by a waymarker post a few paces south of the ruins of Amnodd-wen farm. Climb left just beyond a wall on to rough slopes to the south of a stream. After going through a gap in a cross-wall a grass track climbs to the ridge just north of the main summit.

A variant of this leaves the track by a wall corner at GR 816377 on a grassy high point just north of the ruined farm. Looking up you'll see faint wheel-tracks. Head for these across the easy grass. The wheel-tracks will eventually arc right to go though a gateway at an intersection of walls and join the first-mentioned path above Amnodd-wen at around GR 821374. The mountain can be accessed from the woodlands of Y Lordship in the south-east but the terrain on Lechwedd Erwent is tough and trackless.

RIDGE ROUTE

Moel Llyfnant

Distance: 2¼ miles/3.6km
Height gain: 755ft/230m
Time: 1¼ hours

Head south by the ridge fence, over the south top and down the south ridge, whose terrain after the first steep drop is more peaty and scattered with shallow pools. Keep to the narrow path on the right side of the ridge, passing a couple of those pools before curving right to a primitive stile in a wire fence (GR 824355).

Over this a narrow path descends grass slopes to the broad col between Arenig Fawr and Moel Llyfnant. A short length of wall puts you on the right course to ascend the lower grassy slopes of Moel Llyfnant. On reaching the ridge veer left on open slopes to reach a tumbledown drystone wall, which leads the route to the summit.

Opposite: The path from the col to Arenig Fawr's south ridge.

MOEL YMENYN

Looking at the map Moel Ymenen looks an exciting prospect: beautifully placed for a view of Arenig Fawr's eastern face and with enough crags to make life interesting. But Moel Ymenen is a brute of a hill, guarded by steep slopes, walls and fences with no stiles, and tussocky grass, bracken and deep, ankle-twisting heather. Its majestic neighbour Arenig Fawr is a much easier proposition.

For the walker who likes a challenge and doesn't mind roughing it to get this new perspective of the Arenig, I will give one route.

Opposite: Moel Ymenyn seen across Dolydd Bychain.

Route MA34
Maestron and Dolydd Bychain

A short but rough climb through interesting country

Start: Parking places at lane junction, Maestron (GR: SH 861359)
Distance: 2¼ miles/3.6km
Height gain: 820ft/250m
Time: 1–1½ hours

Take the left fork lane, which crosses pastures on the north side of the Afon Llafar valley. After passing Blaen-y-cwm-isaf farm, the lane ends at the courtyard of the stone-built house, Blaen-y-cwm-uchaf. Go through a gate to the left of the house then follow the top wall across a marshy field.

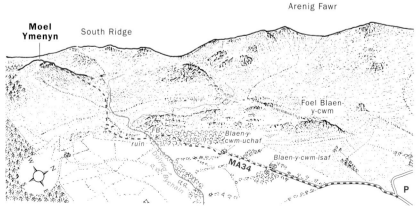

215

After going over a stile on the right into the woods of Maen Ymenyn, turn left down to a footbridge over the lively stream with some attractive waterfalls. Over another ladder stile the path leaves the woods and comes to some old sheepfolds and the ruins of an old small-holding. Ignore the stile on the left and climb past an open country sign.

Above a drystone wall a track leads uphill, heading SSW at first before winding past Craigiau Maesmatthew. Veer right for the stream, Dolydd Bychain, and head up the valley – there's no path and a couple of fences to cross. The steep heather, bracken and crag slopes of Moel Ymenyn rear up on the left and the lower crag and moor grass slopes of Banc y Merddwr close in.

Just beyond Moel Ymenyn's upper crags you'll see an easier line of grass and boulder angling up right. Follow this as it keeps just to the left of a patch of scree to reach the crest just to the west of the summit.

RIDGE ROUTE

Arenig Fawr
Distance: 2¼ miles/3.8km
Height gain: 1250ft/380m
Time: 1½–2 hours

From the summit head west across rough slopes to pass a small pool. Now you need to work your way north-west towards the top of the hollow of Dolydd Bychain. Cross the stream and climb the crag-studded grass slopes to the point where the nearby fence bends north on to the lower slopes of Arenig Fawr's south ridge. Soon you'll join a narrow path that climbs all the way to Craig y Bychau at the tip of the south ridge. Now most of the hard work is done.

Follow the broad lake-scattered ridge, by the ridge fence at first. At a primitive stile in the fence (GR 824355) the path curves right, easing away from the fence. After passing a couple more little lakes it confronts the steep slopes of Arenig Fawr's south top. The ridge fence has now rejoined your course and you follow it all the way to the rocks of the south top, and onwards to the memorial and shelter of the higher north top.

Opposite: Crossing Dolydd Bychain en route to Moel Ymenyn.

Moel Llyfnant lies in the central Arenig flanked in the east by the bigger Arenig Fawr and overlooking the wild but beautiful valley of the Lliw, which flows away south to meet the River Dee. It is connected to Arenig Fawr by a high marshy saddle of land and throws out a wide soggy ridge to Moel y Slates on the Foel Boeth ridge.

Although it's a fine shapely peak, Moel Llyfnant is completely overshadowed by Arenig Fawr when seen from the north. But when you take that little mountain road linking Trawsfynydd and Bala and you stop in the lonely valley of Blaen Lliw, it's the smaller peak's turn to be king. From here Arenig gets a bit scruffy – it's a bit of a vagabond with dishevelled moorland slopes.

Llyfnant, however, is a powerfully shaped cone, scraped with scree and lined by crags and outcrops. Most walkers from this direction will not be able to resist the fierce but inviting challenge issued by these steep southern slopes. Arenig Fawr will have to wait.

The summit itself is splendid: firm grass, lots of crag and there's even a mini Castle of the Winds on the south edge. You have to squeeze past these spiky rocks on the routes up and down the south ridge. The remains of a small manganese mine lie just below the summit at GR 808350 with a visible entrance to a level and a filled-in shaft, while the shells of two old mine buildings lie crumbling into nearby rocks.

The views from the summit are dominated by Arenig Fawr to the east, although the northern skyline is fascinating – you can trace peaks from Holyhead Mountain on Anglesey, through the Llyn Peninsula, to Snowdon, the Glyderau and the Carneddau. Only the big Arenig can better this.

Opposite: Moel Llyfnant's southern slopes.
Right: Moel Llyfnant from Blaen Lliw.

Route MA35
Pont Rhyd-y-fen and Amnodd-wen
The most popular route – if a little dull

Start: Pont Rhyd-y-fen, park at junction of
 A4212 and B4391 (GR: SH 816395)

Distance: 4 miles/6.6km

Height gain: 1445ft/440m

Time: 2½ hours

From the car park, cross the busy A-road on to the narrow Arenig lane descending to the bridge, Pont Rhyd-y-fen, which lies beneath the crags of a nearby quarry and those of Daear Fawr above. A short way beyond the bridge turn right on to a stony track, which runs parallel to the old railway trackbed for a while before climbing left past an old quarry.

Beyond a ladder stile in a cross-wall the track becomes waterlogged and submerged with rushes until it reaches the substantial ruins of Amnodd-wen. Beyond this it becomes a beautifully firm grass track climb-ing to the col between Moel Llyfnant and Arenig Fawr. Both mountains are fully visible and the landscapes are truly magnificent.

The track ends at the col but a faint path crosses the col. It's just a simple matter of climbing the grass slopes of Moel Llyfnant, initially following the line of an old wall westwards to the ridge before turning left for the trig point on the summit.

Descent
From the summit follow the wall and fence northwards. The fence and wall part com-pany and the route follows the latter slightly east of north before veering right in a direct line towards the broad col between Moel Llyfnant and Arenig Fawr's south ridge. Make your way down easy grass slopes where you should join a short stretch of wall down to the col. Here, a faint path leads to the main track north to Pont Rhyd-y-fen.

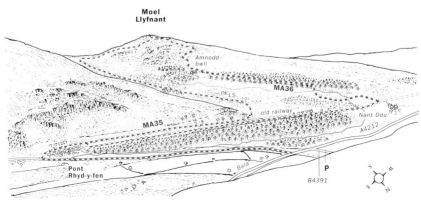

Route MA36

Amnodd-bwll and the North Ridge

Perhaps the easiest route with fine views of Arenig Fawr

Start: Pont Rhyd-y-fen: park at junction of A4212 and B4391 (GR: SH 816395)

Distance: 4 miles/6.5km

Height gain: 1430ft/435m

Time: 2¼ hours

Cross the busy A-road from the car park before turning off on the narrow Arenig lane descending to Pont Rhyd-y-fen. A short way beyond the bridge turn right on to a stony track. When you see the grassy trackbed of the old railway on your right descend to it and follow it westwards. In places it is delightful, in others marshy – you'll need to climb to the banks of the cuttings where this is the case.

Below: On the old Arenig railway track.

On reaching the stony forestry track across a ladder stile and a gate, turn left and follow it up the valley to the ruins of Amnodd-bwll. (Note that the line of the public footpath doesn't exist on the ground and is blocked by the forestry plantations at GR 806377 so walkers have kept to the track).

Beyond Amnodd-bwll a delightful grass track winds up the northern slopes of Moel Llyfnant before ending just short of a ravine. There are no paths hereabouts but the best way for terrain and views is to rake half-left to reach the broad shoulder of the north ridge and then climb south to a subsidiary rocky top. A faint track now heads for the cairn on the main summit, passing through a gap in a tumbledown wall en route.

Descent

The best way is to descend north over the subsidiary top and down to a tumbledown wall-corner at GR 807361, then descend north-west to the track-end. The track, in turn, leads to the old railway trackbed, where you should turn right. A white arrow directs you to the right as the railway trackbed gets entangled with scrubby woods. The stony track you're directed to leads out to the road just east of Pont Rhyd-y-fen.

Right: On Moel Llyfnant's summit.

Route MA37
Pont Blaen Lliw

A rough route but the climb is stimulating
Start: Parking area at Pont Blaen Lliw
  (GR: SH 803336)
Distance: 1¾ miles/2.8km
Height gain: 1180ft/360m
Time: 2 hours

Climb eastwards from the bridge along a narrow lane before turning left down the drive of Hendre Blaen-lliw. Take the right fork track that keeps the house to the left before swinging right towards rough moorland. Ignore the left fork track instead continuing east, then north-east towards the moorland with the slopes of Moel Llyfnant rearing up to the left. The track fades as it bends left to reach a cross-wall.

Beyond this there's no trace of the path marked on the map and what appear to be paths are the lines of old drainage ditches. The best way is to climb left away from the tussocky valley floor to the higher firmer ground at the foot of Moel Llyfnant. Eventually you come to the foot of Llyfnant's south ridge, a place marked by rashes of scree.

There's still no path but the course is very straightforward if somewhat steep. You will come to a fence corner. Keep the fence to your right and continue up the grassy nose of the hill, keeping the roughest screes to the left. Squeeze between an impressive outcrop of spiky rocks and the fence and climb to a prominent outcrop that marks the southern edge of the mountain – it's a great viewpoint and an excellent lunch stop. The cairned summit lies a short way north.

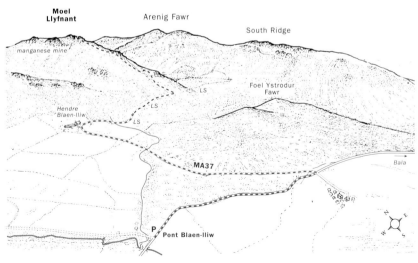

Other route options

You could start on the old railway trackbed east of Llyn Tryweryn (GR 792384) then leave it beyond the Penllyn Forest spruce plantations to climb by a fence up a ridge of tussocky grass. The route would then join the ridge route from Moel y Slates and climb the slopes of Lechwedd Rudd to Moel Llyfnant's summit.

LINK ROUTES

Moel y Slates

Distance: 1¾ miles/2.8km
Height gain: 150ft/ 45m
Time: 1 hour

Head northwards along the summit crest before following the fence left down the rough grass slopes of Lechwedd Rudd. Heather and tussocky grass take hold as you follow the northern perimeter of a spruce forest to a moorland col, which more often than not is a little marshy. The route continues in similar fashion as it climbs by the fence to the grassy summit of Moel y Slates.

Arenig Fawr

Distance: 2¼ miles/3.6km
Height gain: 1080ft/330m
Time: 1½ hours

From the summit follow the wall and fence northwards. The fence and wall part company and the route follows the latter slightly east of north before veering right in a direct line towards the broad col between Moel Llyfnant and Arenig Fawr's south ridge. Make your way down easy grass slopes where you should join a short stretch of wall down to the col.

A clear if damp path crosses the col. Ignore the right fork, but stay with the narrow path that climbs the western flanks of Arenig's south ridge to a primitive stile over a cross-fence. The path gradually curves left to pass several shallow pools before confronting the steep slopes leading to Arenig Fawr's south top. By now the fence you crossed earlier has rejoined the path. Follow it up the steep slopes, past the rock outcrops of the south top and onwards to the main north top.

Right: Crossing the col to climb Moel Llyfnant's east flank.

Dduallt, the black heights, is perhaps the most isolated of all the 2000ft/600m peaks in Snowdonia. An ascent of Dduallt more often than not means struggling through rough heather or marshy grassland for at least some of the way.

The mountain can be forgiven for being wet in places. The flat marshy ground to the east gives birth to two great rivers: the Dee, known as the Dyfrdwy in these parts, and the Mawddach, a sublimely beautiful river, which flows down to its estuary at Barmouth. The Eiddon, Fwy and Mynach streams also cut rocky furrows into an extremely complex range of craggy knolls and forestry plantations. The last-mentioned add considerably to the navigational problems, especially as few of tracks are shown on current OS maps.

I'll now tell you what's good about Dduallt, and there's a lot that *is* good. Some of it lies in the heart and soul rather than in cold logic. Dduallt is tranquil and lonely for a start, and there are no signs of path erosion – actually there are not many paths to be eroded. The landscapes are big with wide skies and little-known views of nearby crags and distant well-remembered peaks.

Just as the map promises, the east face, known as Daear Sinc, is craggy and precipitous: it's a bit like the top of Tryfan with its sheer rock buttresses jutting out from this wide, flat plateau of heather and moss like an upturned ship's hull. Though the surrounding terrain can be difficult, both the north and south ridges are a joy to walk on – they're both a mixture of short grasses and bilberry, interspersed with volcanic dolerite crags and outcrops.

The summit has a tiny cairn perched on one of these outcrops and from it you can see most of Snowdonia. The Aran and Cadair Idris ranges are seen to particularly good advantage. The CROW Act has been especially kind to Dduallt and has opened up many new ways, ones visiting those little-known corners – Carreg Lusog, which apes Dduallt; Craig y Llestri, a craggy outcrop, which defies its modest height; and Cyfyng y Benglog, where the Afon Eiddon cuts itself an exciting gorge between Craig y Benglog and Foel Ddu. I hope by now I've persuaded you to find your best boots and your map of the Arenig.

Opposite: Dduallt's summit rocks.

Route MA38

Cwm yr Allt-lwyd and the north ridge

A splendid high-level route

Start: Cwm yr Allt-lwyd – car parking at the tight road bend (GR: SH 788292)

Distance: 3 miles/4.8km

Height gain: 1440ft/440m

Time: 1¼–2 hours

Follow the tarred farm drive over the bridge spanning the infant Mawddach and onwards to the gate fronting Cwm-hasgen farm. Don't go through the gate but turn right and head across a field towards a metal gate. Go over the step stile by the gate and head east to follow a faint path alongside a fence. This skirts the lower hillside of Allt Lwyd. There is no access to the well-defined track on the other side of the fence until the gate at GR 794292.

After going through the gate stay with this track. Just before the currently uninhabited farmhouse of Allt-lwyd take the upper left fork in tracks, which avoids an unnecessary descent into the valley. The track now rakes up the wilder slopes of Ffridd Bach before fording the Mawddach. Often the ford is too deep for walkers and you will probably have to continue to the plateau at Waun y Griafolen (around GR 811293) before tackling the north ridge. A wire fence acts as a guide as you climb the rough, but not too rough, grassy rock-studded slopes all the way to the summit.

Opposite: In Cwm yr Allt-llwyd.
Overleaf: Crossing the Mawddach with Dduallt's north ridge ahead.

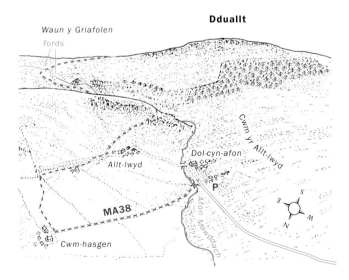

228

Route MA39

Rhydymain and the south ridge

A long route using country lanes, forest tracks and pathless hillslopes

Start: Rhydymain – car park opposite village hall (GR: SH 805221)

Distance: 4¼ miles/7.6km

Height gain: 1900ft/565m

Time: 2½ hours

From the car park follow the lane towards the village centre, past the village hall. Just beyond the left-hand bend take the first road on the right, then leave that for a track climbing left from behind the large chapel. This beautiful track rakes across wooded hill-slopes above the rooftops before reaching a high lane.

Turn right along this, then right again at the next T-junction (there are spaces for a few cars here if you need to save half a mile). The road climbs towards the southern edge of a conifer forest, which fills the hollow between Rhobell Fawr and its neighbour Dduallt. Take the right fork at the road-end to enter the forest. Ignore all turn-off tracks and head northwards with the main flinted forestry road.

After a mile or so the track comes to the western perimeter of the forest with the rugged slopes of Rhobell Fawr rising up to the left. At GR 799258 you'll see a clearing

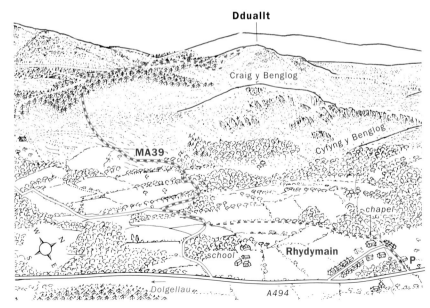

Above: Exiting from the forest on the climb to Dduallt head.

on the right where the cottage Ty-newydd-y-mynydd used to stand, and a footpath way-marker post. Here leave the main track for a grassy, sometimes marshy forest ride that angles slightly right north-east through the trees.

At its terminus turn right to follow a much narrower track that tucks under the trees. The terrain is now one of pine needles and occasional muddy patches. This track is becoming rather overgrown as it nears the eastern edge of the forest and you'll need to limbo dance under some of the fallen trees. At the exit (GR 805259) at a corner in the plantation's edge go over a step-stile in the fence before following the fence to the left.

A narrow undulating path begins from another step-stile on the left and follows the rough terrain on the east side of the forest, with the crag and grass slopes of Dduallt rising beyond a marshy hollow. At the head of this hollow climb north-east on pathless slopes to join Dduallt's south ridge, which is a delightful mix of grass, bilberry, a little heather and a scattering of shallow peaty pools.

Descent

Descend the south ridge for about 300 yards/m before heading south-west down pathless grassy hillslopes aiming from the forestry corner at GR 808269. (If you go too far along the south ridge you will have to cross a small valley created by a stream.) A narrow path, rough at times, follows an undulating course by the forest's edge.

Go over a step stile at the fence corner at GR 807259 and turn right towards the next forestry corner (GR 805259) where you'll find another step stile. Over this a narrow forest path tucks through the trees. In the early stages it's a bit overgrown and obstructed with fallen trees but things soon improve. The path comes to a wide forest ride. Turn left along it, then left again on a stony forest track, which continues southwards to the southern tip of the plantation.

Winding country lanes now descend through farmed hillslopes, giving exquisite views of the verdant Wnion valley and the craggy Aran ridges beyond. A short way past the right turn at a T-junction, leave the road at GR 798221 for a wonderful green road that rakes left, bound by hedgerow, woodland and pasture, to reach Rhydymain village by its huge chapel.

Below: The summit cairn on Dduallt looking towards Bala.

Route MA40

Pont Fronwydd and the south ridge

A splendid high-level route

Start: Pont Fronwydd – lay-by east of hamlet
(GR: SH 834249)

Distance: 3¼ miles/5.2km

Height gain: 1670ft/510m

Time: 2 hours

There's very little parking in the hamlet and the best place for the car is a lay-by about 400yds/m along the A494 towards Bala. An unsurfaced lane beginning on the west side of the bridge winds past the ruins of Cae'r-dynyn before veering north, with the Afon Mynach to the right, to squeeze between the conifer-cloaked Carreg yr Aderyn (bird's stone) and Moel Glydfa.

Where the stony lane veers right to cross the river leave it for a less prominent track maintaining direction up the valley. It rounds a craggy knoll before coming to a gate on your right marked 'open country'. Go through this and follow a faint path meandering generally westwards to pass through a gap in a tumbledown wall.

By now the rugged, knobbly ridge of Rhobell Fawr dominates the western horizon, with the craggy hollow of Cyfyng y Benglog falling away to the south-west.

The track soon fades among the heather but by heading slightly north of west on the easiest ground you can find (the odd sheep-track will help) you will come across a wooden gate in a fence (GR 817254). This is sited just south of the foot of the ridge to Carreg Lusog, a stony hill at the head of the Mynach cwm.

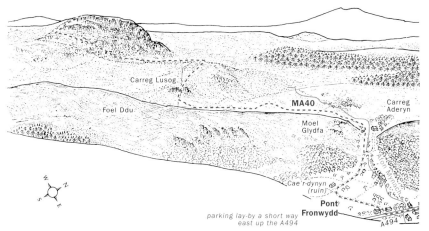

Dduallt

Carreg Lusog

Foel Ddu

MA40

Carreg Aderyn

Moel Glydfa

Cae'r-dynyn (ruin)

Pont Fronwydd

A494

parking lay-by a short way east up the A494

Above: The track from Pont Fronwydd into the hills.

Once through the gate, head north along the ridge, which soon becomes craggy. There are no paths but the going is relatively easy. Beyond Carreg Lusog's summit (GR 818264), a fence promises a short-cut across the low heathery depression between the ridge and that of Dduallt, but the going is very rough, so stay on the high ground of Braich Lusog instead.

Step over the low wire fence at the inter-section on the north summit and follow the north-west bound fence. Where this bends slightly left look out for a shepherds' track around 20yds/m to the north. This offers eas-ier terrain and climbs through heather, grass and mosses parallel to the fence at first.

The fence and path soon tackle Dduallt's craggy east flank. The path swings half-right, away from the fence, then fades on slopes of crag, bilberry and grass. Maintain your north-west direction: the going is easy and it's not far to the south ridge, where you'll pass a few shallow peaty pools before reaching the summit.

Route MA41

Cerrig-yr-lwch and the north ridge

A long but fascinating approach

Start: Pont Dolhendre – space for cars near
    telephone box (GR: SH 854308)

Distance: 4¼ miles/6.8km

Height gain: 1835ft/560m

Time: 2½–3 hours

Go across to the south side of the bridge and
turn right at the crossroads along the lane
marked as a cul-de-sac. The bold crags of
Carn Dochan dominate the early scenes as
the lane climbs past a few houses and fields
clogged with thick bracken and foxgloves.
The lane soon becomes a stony track, which
descends to the borders of the forest of Coed
Bryn Bras.

Here a modern bridge and an old clapper
bridge span the Afon Fwy. Over the modern
bridge the tracks divide. Take the less prominent left fork, which is the footpath shown on
the map. This climbs through the trees to join
another forestry track. Just beyond this take
the right fork, which soon becomes a pine
needle and stone track winding through
really dark forest, giving the aura of a scene
from Hansel and Gretel.

Where the track comes to a vague crossroads, ignore the grassy ride straight ahead
but bear left. Boggy in places at first, this
meanders to a ladder stile on the edge of the
forest (GR 837305).

The track continues through a marshy
upland hollow with the grassy flanks of Marian to the left and the bracken and boulders

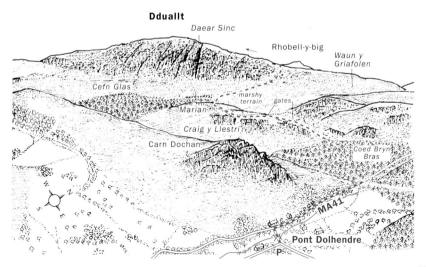

tions of sparse spruce trees. Descend the ridge's western end parallel to the forest. You are now confronted by the great marshy plateau separating you and Dduallt. It gives birth to two rivers, the Mawddach and the Dee, so it's wet in places, really wet. There are no paths but intelligent navigation avoids the worst bogs.

Aim for the lower slopes of the north ridge – ones that can easily be climbed; the fence corner at GR 814287 is a good place to aim for. The continuing fence will guide you up safe slopes of grass and stone all the way to the north ridge. Turn left here and follow faint paths to the little summit cairn.

Other route options

A long and initially very pleasant route begins at Buarthmeini on the Bala–Trawsfynydd mountain road. It follows roughly the line of the Afon Lliw before climbing among crags to Cefn y Griafolen. A long trek now follows southwards across the source of the Mawddach before climbing Dduallt's north ridge. It's also possible to climb from Rhydymain on a route passing Pen-y-rhiw farm to the east before climbing east of the craggy hollow, Cyfyng y Benglog, beyond which you'd meet Route MA40.

RIDGE ROUTE

There is a rather contrived, dull and rough route across the head of the Afon Mawddach to Foel Boeth, but this is not recommended.

of Cerrig Chwibanog to the right. A gate and ladder stile allow progress through the first cross-fence, where Dduallt's dark crags first appear on the horizon. On reaching another gate and step stile in the next cross-fence, the track ends in a bed of rushes.

You could go over the stile and continue across the marshy flatlands to the base of Dduallt's north ridge – the conventional way – but try turning left along the near side of the fence from here to reach a step stile by a fence junction. Go over this and you find yourself walking south-west along the pleasant grassy ridge of Marian with Dduallt straight ahead and the impressive rocky Aran Ridge away to the left. The cheeky little bell-shaped rock peak to the right of Dduallt is Rhobell-y-big.

Marian's grass ridge gives way to the rocky-sided Cerrig-yr-lwch. To the left are planta-

Opposite: The old clapper bridge at the entrance to the forest beneath Carn Dochan.
Below: Dduallt's harsh east face seen across Waun y Griafolen.

A gold mine, precipitous crags and an ancient castle full of mystery and legend: what more can you ask of your hill or mountain? Carn Dochan has all of these, even if it is a peak in miniature – just 1102feet/335m above the sea.

Carn Dochan, one of the outliers of Dduallt, overlooks the Lliw Valley south-west of Llyn Tegid (Bala Lake). Seen from the valley it's quite a spectacular sight, with its fierce crags soaring from fields and woodland. The gold mines, which provided reasonable yields in the nineteenth century, lie high on the south-east side of the hill.

There is dispute over the origins of the castle but many historians believe the stone structures to be thirteenth-century, and probably built for the Princes of Wales. They conclude that the earthworks date back much further in time, probably to the Roman era. The crumbling remains reveal an irregular stone-walled enclosure, a D-shaped southern tower, two further rounded towers, and rectangular central buildings. Standing among the ruins you can feel the impregnability of this cliff-top fortress, because the terrain to the south and west, guarded also by the rock face of Craig y Llestri, is difficult and marshy.

Opposite: Carn Dochan from Dolhendre.
Above: The ramparts of Castell Carndochan.

Route MA42
Dolhendre
A short but fascinating route
Start: Pont Dolhendre (bridge)
    (GR: SH 854308)
Distance: 1 mile/1.6km
Height gain: 490ft/150m
Time: ¼ hour

Go over the bridge spanning the Afon Lliw and continue up the lane to the crossroads. Turn right on the lane marked 'No Through Road'. This passes a few cottages with the crags of Carn Dochan glowering ahead.

On the approach to the forest, Coed Bryn Bras, take the second gate on the left – the one just before the river crossing – to follow a track which snakes up the hillside past a sheepfold. It veers right on the approach to a few larch trees, climbing parallel to the forest's edge and the river before swinging left again. Where the track ends, maintain your direction to reach the ridge, then turn left to the rocks and old fortress on the summit.

Other route options
Footpaths by way of Ty Coch and Tyddyn Ronnen to the east allow access to the rocky knoll of Graig ddu. A simple trek north along the ridge leads to the summit.

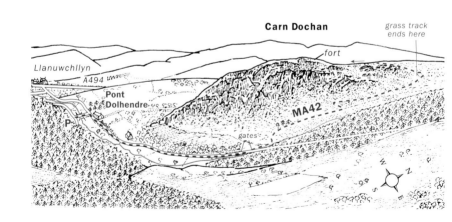

Carn Dochan

grass track ends here

fort

Llanuwchllyn

A494

Pont Dolhendre

P

MA42

gates

Above: The fort on the summit of Carn Dochan with Llyn Tegid in the valley below.

RIDGE ROUTE

Dduallt

Distance: 3¾ miles/6km
Height gain: 1345ft/410m
Time: 2¼ hours

From the fort on Carn Dochan, head south-west along the crest, which is marshy in places, and go through the gate in the first cross-fence. Keep to the right of the prominent peak of Foel y Graig to join a path which has climbed from the farm pastures to the east. This crosses moorland to a footbridge beneath the rugged slopes of Craig y Llestri, where it's a short but steep climb to the summit.

Head westwards by a fence then left over a step stile near the next fence-intersection (GR 833299). Now you continue along the ridges of Marian and Cerrig-yr-lwrch before descending to flat marshes at the foot of Dduallt. Head directly west, at first parallel to the forest on the left. On reaching the fence corner at GR 814287 follow the westbound fence up safe slopes of grass and stone all the way to Dduallt's north ridge. Turn left here and follow faint paths to the summit.

Bridging the gap between the Migneint and the Berwyn and slightly outside Snowdonia, I had considered omitting Foel Goch, but as it is a 2000-footer, I yielded to my peak-bagging instincts.

While Foel Goch, the red bare hill, has no real crags to write home about, its lower ridges and knolls have plenty. The summit, like the rest of the hill, is an amiable place, where short grass is topped by a concrete trig point, a small cairn and a border stone, inscribed with the parish names of Llangwm on one side and Llanfor on the other.

The views from the peak are extensive and encompass the rugged Aran ridge seen across Bala and Llyn Tegid, and further away Cadair Idris and the Arenig. To the north the magnificent Snowdon, Glyderau and Carneddau peaks are all recognisable on the skyline.

One undulating ridge leads west from Foel Goch to Garnedd Fawr and one reaches north to Llangwm in the fertile Medrad Valley, while a short steep spur descends south to Moel Darren. The latter divides the corries of Cwm Da and Nant Cefn-coch. A third ridge stretches east over Orddu to the outlier Pen y Cerrig-serth. Orddu sends out yet another ridge, Bryn Bras, which is perhaps the finest of the Foel Goch group for it is knobbly and studded with crag. Bryn Bras provides the finest approach to the main mountain.

Opposite: The summit of Foel Goch.

Route MA43
Bryn Bras and Orddu

A very pleasant ridge route with fine views

Start: Coed-y-bedo – limited roadside
    parking at start of the walk at SH 966405
    or on corner of minor road to the south
    (GR: SH 963395)

Distance: 2½ miles/4km

Height gain: 1150ft/350m

Time: 1½ hours

Cwm Main is very pretty with bracken-cloaked craggy hillsides and pastures. Unfortunately a line of pylons tempers the beauty, but perhaps only for photographers. The more easterly of two cottages is Coed-y-bedo farm, once home to the fifteenth-century Welsh poet Bedo Aeddren. The footpath wanted here is the one to the north-east of the farmhouses at GR 966405.

Go through the gate on the north side of the road by the footpath signpost and follow the right field edge to a stile at the top corner. Over the stile turn right on a cart track, which skirts the northern side of a craggy hillock. Just to the right here you'll see the crumbling ruins of an old stone building where cock fighting took place.

Watch out for a junction, where you turn right uphill. It's a fine way to the ridge of Bryn Bras and the views widen as height is gained. To the east the Berwyn ridges stretch beyond the wide flat pastures of the Dee, while in the south the Aran rise majestically from the waters of Llyn Tegid, Snowdonia's largest natural lake. Soon the twin peaks of Arenig Fawr peep up from behind Foel Goch's south ridge and Foel Goch looms large at the end of the tussocky grass valley of Cwm Da.

Bryn Bras is a delightful complex of rocky knolls, and the track takes you a good way along it before fading into the tufty grass at some sheepfolds on the left side of the ridge. There are intermittent tracks from here on in and some decisions to be made. It's splendidly worthwhile to climb to the airy rock and grass summits, but a short way beyond the sheepfolds, at a junction of fences (GR 965417), a gate allows you through a fence, which must eventually be crossed. Staying on the ridge means that you will need to climb

over the fence just north of the 536m spot height.

Assuming you went through the gate, a faint track heads northwards before arcing left around the high slopes of Orddu. Go over a step stile in a fence and climb to the border stones on its summit. The fence-side path now continues to the foot of Foel Goch, with the deep hollow of Cwm Llan stretching away to farm pastures surrounding the little village of Llangwm. A prominent vehicle track climbs to the ridge from this direction.

The track wanted now rakes up left. (It is important not to be tricked on to narrow but clear paths which climb straight ahead and right from here.) A couple of small cairns highlight your path, which soon reaches the ridge. An easy path now climbs to the trig point on the summit.

Foel Goch

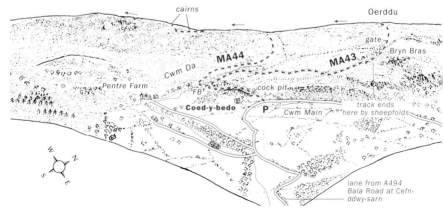

Descent

Leave the summit for the eastern ridge. It would be very easy to continue along Foel Goch's north ridge in error, so it is imperative to descend right on reaching the small cairn a short way east of the trig point. The cairned path descends easily down the hillside to gain Orddu's ridge at the top of the vehicle track from Llangwm. Stay with the ridge fence and border stones until reaching the step stile in the fence at the east side of Orddu's summit.

Now a faint path arcs around the head of Cwm Da towards the knobbly Bryn Bras ridge. It goes through a gate at GR 965417. On the downhill route it is better to follow the fence down right to reach the end of a clear track by some sheepfolds. Follow this down to a track junction near the base of the ridge (GR 960405). Keep left here and follow the track beneath a craggy knoll on the right and alongside a line of pylons. Watch out for a substantial stile on the left as the track turns a corner around the east side of the knoll. Over this stile follow the left side of the fields down to a roadside gate at the walk's finish.

Route MA44
Cwm Da

A rather dull plod

Start: Coed-y-bedo – limited roadside parking at start at SH 966405, or on corner of minor road (GR: SH 963395)

Distance: 2¼ miles/3.5km

Height gain: 1035ft/315m

Time: 1½ hours

As in Route MA43 go through the gate by the footpath signpost to the east of Coed-y-bedo and follow the right field edge to a stile at the top corner. Over the stile turn right on a cart track, which skirts the northern side of a craggy hillock. A short way along the track and to the right you'll see the ruins of an old building where cock fighting took place.

This time ignore the right forking uphill track but instead go straight ahead on a path that soon arcs right through scrub woodland and gorse to cross Nant Cwm Da on a wooden bridge. Cwm Da is quite a stark and brooding sort of place, where rushes are almost as prolific as grass. Tracks, once part of a road linking Llanfor and Llangwm, will come and go, as they sink into the mosses and rushes which surround the stream.

Once over the stream turn right on a track running alongside it. Through a gate the terrain becomes very marshy for a while. Beyond the quagmire a grassy raised bank, the stream still to your right, heads uphill. Soon the rush-filled hollow of the old track appears again but it is prudent to walk the sheep trods to the side.

The going improves as height is gained and the track becomes almost respectably dry as it reaches the col between Orddu and Foel Goch. Here you look down on the farming village of Llangwm. At the col take the wider path raking left up Foel Goch's slopes rather than climbing directly ahead. The path comes to the ridge at a small cairn, where it's just a short easy climb to the summit.

Descent

The key to the early descent is to turn right at the small cairn just east of the summit. This takes you down to the col beneath Orddu. Turn right here along a winding grass track that soon becomes wetter and rush-filled. In later stages Nant Da comes alongside you and guides you to a gate in a cross-fence. Beyond this, watch out for a bridge over the stream on the left.

The succeeding track leads you through a gap between the base of Bryn Bras and a rocky knoll on the right (a line of pylons also runs through the gap). Watch out for a substantial stile on the left as the track turns a corner around the east side of the knoll. Over this follow the left side of the fields down to a roadside gate at the finish of the walk.

Other route options

There are various options from the north side, where the village of Llangwm provides parking. The best of these follows a path from the south west of the village (GR 964444, just south of a T-junction and an old chapel) and climbs across fields to a conifer plantation, before heading SSW above the farm of Ceseilgwm to the edge of the access area to the north of Foel Goch's summit. Various routes from the west take in Garnedd Fawr, although these are longer with more farmland and less hill en route.

RIDGE ROUTE

Garnedd Fawr
Distance: 1¼ miles/2km
Height gain: 150ft/ 45m
Time: 1 hour

A simple grass ridge with little route-finding required. Head west from the summit to reach a fence corner. A ridge fence now leads all the way to the cairn on Garnedd Fawr.

Opposite: Foel Goch from Nant Cwm-da.

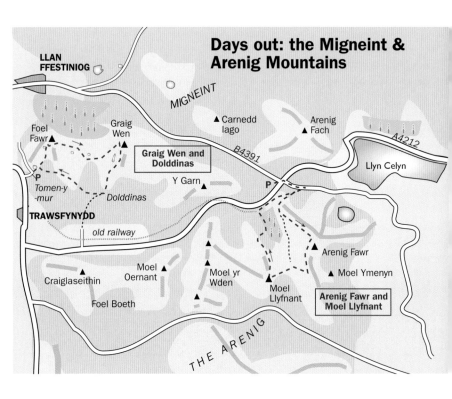

Days out: the Migneint & Arenig Mountains

LLAN FFESTINIOG

MIGNEINT

▲ Carnedd Iago

Arenig
▲ Fach

A4212

Foel Fawr ▲

Graig Wen ▲

B4391

Llyn Celyn

Graig Wen and Dolddinas

Y Garn ▲

P

Tomen-y-mur

Dolddinas

TRAWSFYNYDD

old railway

▲

Arenig Fawr

Craiglaseithin ▲

Moel Oernant ▲

Moel yr Wden ▲

▲ Moel Ymenyn

Foel Boeth

▲

Moel Llyfnant ▲

Arenig Fawr and Moel Llyfnant

THE ARENIG

Opposite: Graig Wen from Foel Fawr.

Days Out: the Migneint & Arenig Mountains

Graig Wen and Dolddinas
A journey across lonely, seldom-visited peaks
Start: Tomen-y-mur car park (GR: SH 708389)
Distance: 6 miles/10km
Height gain: 1180ft/360m
Time: 4 hours

Before setting out on the walk proper it would be a good idea to stroll around Tomen-y-mur, a Roman military settlement including barracks, a bath-house and small amphitheatre, which was probably an arena for weapons training. Sited at a Roman crossroads, the site was occupied well into the second century by the Romans, then taken over by the princes of Gwynedd. It was briefly re-occupied and developed in medieval times by the invading Norman armies of William Rufus. The great castle mound, which is the Tomen, lies at the far corner of the site and is medieval, probably a Norman motte.

From the car park turn right along the road. Where it turns left go straight ahead along the clear quarry track heading east across grassy moor to pass Llyn yr Oerfel and the fields of Tir-y-mynydd farm. The straw-coloured moorland ridges of Foel Fawr fill the skyline ahead.

About 100 yards/m past the farm turn-off track, leave the quarry track for a rutted route veering slightly left up a grassy hillside

towards the ridge ahead. Below you are the gaunt skeletons of old quarry barracks. A small moorland tarn comes into view on the ridge ahead but the path swings left (north) to climb beneath the crest of the main ridge.

Soon you'll see the breached stone dams of two small reservoirs on the right, which today contain little water. The path disappears into the rushes for a short way but continue northwards through a hollow, keeping the marshiest ground to the right. The path resumes and

takes the route alongside Llyn Craig-y-tan. The largish tarn with a few small islands has a wonderful view of Ffestiniog with the rugged Moelwyn range and its quarries and forests prominent, and the Snowdon range behind.

Paths on the ground have disappeared now but turn right (east) to climb grassy slopes scattered with boulders. You should reach another small tarn, where the rock-fringed summit of Foel Fawr comes into view ahead. Follow a crag-interspersed ridge to the right of the hollow beneath the peak to a point where it levels off. It's now a simple matter of climbing left to the summit cairn.

The ground to the east is undulating with a complex of grassy mounds and marsh-surrounded tarns. The route is now heading for Graig Wen, a slightly higher crag-scattered moor to the east. There's no real path to it, but you cannot go far wrong by following the line of the highest ground parallel to the spruce forest on the left.

By descending east you will pick up a grass track at GR 730396 just west of one of those tarns (the track is marked by black dashes on the OS Explorer map). Follow this south-eastwards to cross a stone-built causeway that was once a reservoir dam. The track disappears, but by aiming north-eastwards across grassland you'll be able to round the north side of the largest of the lakes, Llyn y Graig Wen, before climbing on craggy grass slopes to the ridge. A right turn along the crest brings the route to the small cairn on Graig Wen's summit.

Descend south-westwards down grass slopes to avoid the steepest ground and the crags overlooking Llyn y Graig Wen. You'll soon see the dam/causeway on the south shore, where you'll cross the outflow stream.

Straddle the rocky knoll beyond the dam, then descend left where you should pick up the line of an old water leat (dry these days). This leads you back towards the outflow and to another leat, which should be followed to the right.

Wheel-tracks then lead down the hill towards the green fields of Dolddinas, where you should spot the earthworks of the old Roman practice works. Just before reaching those fields the track meets an old stony track at the apex of a bend. Return to this point after exploring the practice works. These would have been in use for training purposes in the first and second centuries AD by the soldiers of Tomen-y-mur.

Returning to the apex of the bend, ignore the stony track for a less well-defined track, the leftmost of three (the right-hand one is the one you came down on). Follow this across a moorland plateau to the corner of the pastures of Dolbelydr. Just beyond this leave the track for one half-right across the grassy hillslopes. The track climbs over the shoulder of the moor before descending past an active quarry. Beyond this it meets the outward route near Tir-y-mynydd farm and Llyn yr Oerfel. Retrace your steps to the start.

Opposite: Rhinogydd and Llyn Trawsfynydd from near Tomen-y-mur.

Arenig Fawr and Moel Llyfnan

The classic Arenig journey with a couple of twists

Start: Pont Rhyd-y-fen: park at junction of
A4212 and B4391 (GR: SH 816395)

Distance: 9½ miles/15km

Height gain: 2625ft/800m

Time: 6–7 hours

Below you in the valley, the Afon Tryweryn meanders its way through the Arenig on its peaceful way towards Bala and the River Dee. Down the road the expansive waters of Llyn Celyn reflect blue where the little village of Capel Tryweryn used to be. Travel writer George Borrow came here after a long journey over the Migneint. He spied the little riverside farmhouse of Rhyd-y-fen, then a hostelry, and stopped off for ale and a bite to eat.

Behind the farm and beyond the Tryweryn lie two fine mountains: Arenig Fawr with its distinctive twin peaks, and Moel Llyfnant, a craggy escarpment rising from a spread of conifers. It's in that direction we'll head.

Across the busy Trawsfynydd road a narrow lane (Arenig Road) descends to cross the river bridge before heading towards the huge quarry face scarring the northern end of Arenig Fawr. The old railway, which at one time linked Bala with Blaenau Ffestiniog, crosses just beyond the river but its initial course on the right is blocked with thick scrub woods. Just beyond the track, however, a stony farm track leads the route beneath crags and thorn bushes scattered across the northern slopes. Soon the railway track emerges from the trees as a green highway used by walkers, and the return route, but for now stick with the farm track.

The going has been easy so far but suddenly the track gets lost in rushes. Ignore the ladder stile ahead but instead look to the skyline on the left. You are at the base of Arenig Fawr's north-west ridge and you can see a substantial drystone wall which will guide you for most of the climb up it. The rushes persist on the lower regions of the ridge and, although wheel-tracks cross them in the right direction, it's an inauspicious start. Soon, however, the route nears the wall on the right and the rushes are replaced by tufty grass. A good path now begins.

The ridge becomes more spectacular as height is gained. Beyond a gap near a wall junction the path switches to the right side and a new wire fence begins. The ridge is now rocky and soon gets quite steep, but not frighteningly so. Soon you're standing on the ridge top looking right to the main summit. The fence now heads off left.

If you want to make a detour to see the waters and rocky corrie of Llyn Arenig Fawr, divert left for a short way, then head westwards to the 684m spot height at Bwlch Blaen-y-nant. Return to the fence corner at the top of the north-west ridge.

The old wall that used to span the ridge here has all but disappeared into the hillside, but the ground is now firm and rocky and the way ahead is straightforward and, if visibility is good, you can see the summit trig and

Above: On the north-west ridge of Arenig Fawr.

shelter capping the conical summit. If visibility is bad and you still want to continue, head south keeping to the highest ground, then change to a south-westerly direction after about 200 yards/m, still keeping to the crest of the ridge.

The summit has a shelter, a concrete trig point and a memorial plaque to the eight crewmen of a US Air Force B-17 Flying Fortress, who in 1943 were instantly killed when the war-plane, caught in thick fog, crashed into the crags just below the summit.

Bits of wreckage can still be seen strewn across the mountain slopes.

Being higher than anything for miles around, Arenig Fawr enjoys wonderful views. Cadair Idris, the Rhinogydd, Snowdon, the Moelwynion and the Aran mountains are ringed around a misty blue horizon, interrupted only by stretches of the glimmering sea.

The ridge walk continues south, with a fence leading the route down, then up to the rocks on the south peak, where the south ridge slinks away towards the anonymous but fascinating peaks of the upper Mawddach. The south ridge is much lower and less defined, but is enhanced by an abundance of shallow tarns lying between a complex of rocky bluffs.

Now there's a steep descent to the south ridge. Again a fence will act as a guide, but not far past the first of the lakes, it leaves the ridge to traverse the high western slopes. Keep to the west side of the ridge here on a narrow path which eventually arcs right to rejoin the fence at a primitive stile (GR 824355). Once over it the narrow path descends grass slopes to the damp, mossy col beneath Moel Llyfnant.

The path crosses the col then climbs on to Moel Llyfnant's slopes by the side of a crumbling wall. Where the wall ends continue climbing in the same direction up grassy slopes. The faint path arcs left to reach the crest, where easy grass slopes lead south to the spiky rocks of the summit. Moel Llyfnant's summit is a joy, with plenty of rocky perches to take in the views – Arenig Fawr looks

resplendent from here – and there's plenty of soft tufty grass on which to make yourself comfortable with a cup of warming coffee and a sandwich, in the knowledge that there's no more climbing to do.

After you've had your rest, descend northwards past a rocky outcrop, then veer NNW down grassy slopes. At GR 807361 you'll come across some old walls on the right. Follow these down into a shallow grassy ravine where you'll pick up an old mine track, which zigzags down the hillside to pass the ruined cottage of Amnodd-bwll before entering the conifer forest. The track continues through the forest and exits near the ruins of Yr Orsedd.

On reaching the old railway trackbed beyond this turn right. The old railway leads delightfully, if a little damply in places, for most of the way back towards Pont Rhyd-y-fen. A white arrow waymarker points to the right as the track reaches the point where it is choked with scrub woods and you join the outward track just short of the Arenig Road, where you turn left back to the car park.

Left: The sad ruins of Amnodd-bwll with Arenig Fawr behind.
Opposite: The summit cairn on Moel Llyfnant with Arenig Fawr behind.

The Berwyn Mountains

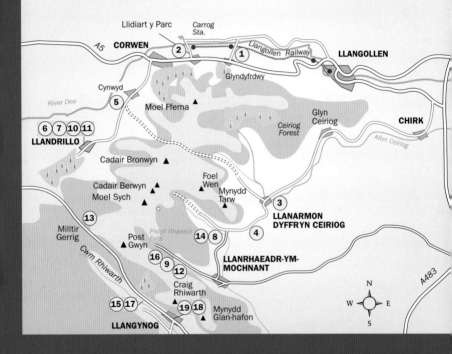

Rising from the green valleys of Denbighshire and the red earth of Shropshire, the Berwyn Mountains form part of a series of long mountain ridges stretching south-westwards to the shores of Llyn Tegid (Bala Lake). Strictly, only the south-western 'Bala' peaks, often known as the Hirnants, are in Snowdonia: the high Berwyn is outside the boundaries, but they're far too important a range to omit on such a technicality.

THE PEAKS

Main Tops	height	
Cadair Berwyn	2722ft	830m
Moel Sych	2713ft	827m
Cadair Bronwen	2572ft	784m
Mynydd Tarw	2233ft	681m
Post Gwyn	2181ft	665m
Moel Fferna	2066ft	630m
Mynydd Glan-hafon	1994ft	608m
Craig Rhiwarth	1745ft	532m

Spanning some 15½ miles/25km from Llangollen to the head of Cwm Rhiwarth above Llangynog, the high Berwyn are bound into parcels by the Dee, Ceiriog, Efyrnwy and Tanat valleys. The range has been designated as both a SSSI (Special Site of Scientific Interest) and SAC (Special Area of Conservation) for this is the largest tract of heather moorland in Wales.

The poor acidic soils of the high ridges are largely cloaked with heather and bilberry, but they're also one of the few places in Wales where the cloudberry grows. These shrubs, not unlike a bramble but lacking thorns, cling closely to the ground with sparse, raspberry-like fruits. Almost as hard to spot is the lesser twayblade, as it's masked by the heather shoots it chooses for its bedfellows. This 2in/5cm-high orchid has tiny red flowers and heart-shaped leaves. It blooms between June and August. Look for it on the damp acid moorland, where you should also find the insect-eating sundew and butterwort.

Above: Looking down Nant y Llyn with the top of Pistyll Rhaeadr just visible in the tree-hung cliffs on the left.

The vegetation has also made the Berwyn attractive to many upland birds including the red and black grouse, the merlin, hen harrier, peregrine falcon and golden plover. I've also seen ring ouzel and the occasional red kite here. Red squirrels inhabit the woodland above Cynwyd and Glyndyfrdwy.

The Countryside Rights of Way (CROW) Act has helped open up some of the more difficult areas of the range, although some strange decisions mean that there are some islands of access, so you'll have to take a helicopter there to enjoy the freedom to roam.

In the high central regions of the range the moors become mountains, with crags and glacial cwms carved from their eastern faces. Moel Sych and Cadair Berwyn together cradle a small tarn, Llyn Lluncaws. For years it was believed by the walking fraternity that Moel Sych was the highest Berwyn at 2713ft – both Moel Sych and Cadair Berwyn's north top had a metric measurement of 827m. However, visitors were puzzled when they looked across to Cadair Berwyn's south top, a splendid rocky diadem, for it appeared to be higher than both of those. Sure enough, when the Ordnance Survey checked their larger-scale maps, it was revealed that the south top reached a height of 830m. Moel Sych, a very much inferior rounded summit, was promptly relegated.

The craggy theme continues on the eastern face to the head of the cwm of the Afon Rhaeadr. Here you'll find Pistyll Rhaeadr, one of the Seven Wonders of Wales, where the Afon Disgynfa tumbles 250ft/76m from the marshy wilderness of its glacial hanging valley, down tree-hung cliffs into the shadows of Tan-y-pistyll. The powerful white-water cascade dwarfs the little Welsh slate farmhouse at its foot. Most wonderfully this farm is also a café and B&B, just waiting to serve hungry walkers.

Some of the Berwyn's appeal lies in the beauty of the surrounding valleys. David Lloyd George, the last Liberal Prime Minister of Britain, described the Ceiriog Valley as 'a piece of heaven that has fallen to earth'. Although in Lloyd George's time there were plans to flood the valley to form a large reservoir, they were resisted and the valley remains as unspoiled today as it was then, with the beautiful river meandering through woodland and rolling verdant hillside pastureland.

In 1165 the well-armed troops of King Henry II marched this way to subdue the rebellious Owain Gwynedd, then Prince of North Wales. At first they repelled the Welsh, who attacked strongly from the lower valley's thick woodland. Forcing their way relentlessly towards the Berwyn ridge, victory seemed inevitable, but suddenly the mountain storms that had been brewing on the high ridges whipped themselves into a black fury. Pounded by great gales and torrential rain, the English floundered in the peat bogs. Believing that the wicked Welsh prince had conjured this great storm with evil wizardry, they retreated.

In the late fourteenth and early fifteenth centuries, the Welsh Prince Owain Glyndwr had two abodes in the Berwyns, one at Llidiart y Parc, near Glyndyfrdwy in the Dee Valley, the other at Sycharth, a remote motte-and-bailey castle in the valley of the Cynllaith, west of Oswestry. Locals will also have you believe that King Arthur had his round table on Cadair Bronwen, one of the Berwyn's big three, so you can imagine that wherever you walk in the Berwyn you're probably following in the foot-steps of great warriors, princes and kings.

Llangynog, once a thriving lead-mining and slate-quarrying village, lies at the confluence of the Afon Eirth and the Afon Tanat and is sheltered by steep hillsides at the foot of the Milltir Gerrig mountain pass. It was the western terminus of the Tanat Valley Light Railway (Oswestry–Llynclys–Llangynog), which opened in 1904 but closed to passengers in 1951. Craig Rhiwarth, the Berwyn's craggiest hill, soars from behind, the village displaying the vivid colours of bracken and gorse, tempered by the steely grey of screes and the dark crags. Beneath Craig Rhiwarth's eastern slopes, Cwm Glan-hafon is the gateway to the highest Berwyn peaks by way of Pistyll Rhaeadr.

Opposite: On a wintry Berwyn ridge.
Overleaf: Moel Sych and Llyn Lluncaws.

The most northerly of the Berwyn 2000-ers, Moel Fferna has no great mountain form. It's a rounded hump of heather moorland rising, ever so gradually, from a long heather ridge overlooking the fields and forests of the Dee Valley.

The mountain was once the hardest to reach. Tales of walkers being turned back by gamekeepers were common – because, along with Vivod Mountain, Moel Fferna is part of an extensive grouse moor. The footpaths disappeared with lack of use into the heather and mosses, and most walkers had difficulty finding routes to the top. The Countryside Rights of Way Act changed all that and now several routes from the valleys are even waymarked by North Berwyn Way signs.

While Moel Fferna isn't exactly a spectacular place, the views from it are wide-sweeping and make the trek well worth the effort. The celebrated peaks of Snowdonia ring around the horizon, along with the Clwydian and Llantysilio ranges. The trig point shown on earlier maps is long gone, although the summit wind shelter, which offers good protection when the weather is unkind, remains.

Those who make the ascent will at some time or other come across the relics of slate mining and quarrying. Spoil heaps and crumbling buildings are all that remain of the Moel Fferna slate mine, which lies high on the mountain's north-east slopes.

Those who use Route B1 will also come across Nant y Pandy Mill deep in the shadows of the woods. Here the powers of the stream were harnessed to cut blocks of slate excavated from the mid-level Deeside Slab Quarry into slabs used in the brewing and building industry, and also for operating tables for hospitals and gravestones. The slate was taken down the mountain on a horse-drawn tramway to the railway station at Glyndyfrdwy on the Ruabon and Barmouth line (which closed in 1968), from where it was transported to all parts of the world.

The current Llangollen Railway had become a popular tourist attraction by the time the line was extended from Llangollen to Carrog near Corwen. Walkers intending to tackle Moel Fferna and perhaps the nearby Vivod Mountain, which has a Bronze Age burial mound on the summit, can link their route by catching one of the trains either from Carrog or Glyndyfrdwy. Travelling on one of the old 'blood and custard' British Rail carriages pulled by an old Great Western steam express is a great experience.

Opposite: Approaching Moel Fferna from the east.

Route B1
Nant y Pandy and Cwm Canol
Follow old quarry tracks
Start: Glyndyfrdwy (GR: SJ 148427)
Distance: 4¼ miles/7km
Height gain: 1670ft/510m
Time: 2½ hours

The route begins on a streamside track on the south side of the A5 and opposite the road to the railway station. The track is marked with a North Berwyn Way waymarker, the first of many you'll see throughout the day, and signed to Nant y Pandy. The stony track passes through woodland. Ignore the left fork track climbing out of the valley but stay with the stony track passing through woodland close to the stream.

Beyond a cottage the route crosses a footbridge, after which a path continues along

Above: The bridge by the mill at Nant y Pandy.
Opposite: Looking back down Route B2 from near the summit of Moel Fferna.

Moel Fferna

Ceiriog Forest

B1

slab quarry

old mill

FB

FB

Coed Ty'n-y-celyn

Glyndyfrdwy
station

River Dee

Llangollen Railway (steam)

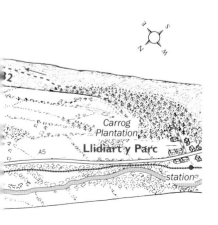

the west side of the stream, passing close to a second cottage before coming across the remains of old slate quarries. Here the path follows part of an old tramway linking the slate mines of Moel Fferna with the old Ruabon to Barmouth railway at Glyndyfrdwy.

Beyond some waterfalls the path re-crosses the stream on a slate bridge with wooden rails and soon joins a stony track, which passes two cottages. Where the track arcs right across fields leave it for a signed path on the left. The narrow path stays low in the valley at first, traversing slopes of bracken before climbing left to join a tarred lane.

Turn right along this to reach the Moel Fferna–Vivod Mountain ridge, where a right turn along a heavily rutted track takes you alongside the conifers of the Ceiriog Forest at first, then along a peat and heather ridge. The views north are dominated by the heathery ridge of the Llantysilio Mountains, which stretch along the north side of the Dee Valley, and the more distant Clwydians, which lead the eye to the North Wales coastline.

The rutted track forges its way towards Moel Fferna, a rather nondescript sort of hill from here, but soon the landscape becomes wilder and more stimulating. On the left the ground falls away in the sullen wilderness of the Ceiriog-ddu valley, a scene overlooked by the crags of the high Berwyn. A gaunt cluster of dead trees adds drama to the scene – all it needs is a couple of soaring vultures to complete the mood. Ignore the North Berwyn Way sign pointing downhill and right but stay with the ridge, before climbing right on a peaty path to the wind shelter on Moel Fferna's summit.

Left: The valley of Nant y Pandy and the village of Glyndyfrdwy.

Route B2
Llidiart y Parc and the Carrog Plantation

*A well waymarked route that could be used
with Route B1*

Start: Llidiart y Parc (GR: SJ 119434)
Distance: 2¾ miles/4.5km
Height gain: 1610ft/490m
Time: 1½ hours

Head south on a lane opposite to the Carrog
turn-off on the A5 then take the track to the
right of Park Grove house. After passing a
couple of cottages and game bird-rearing
pens, follow the North Berwyn Way signs
pointing left into Carrog Plantation. A winding path leads up to a stony track. Immediately opposite the waymarked route climbs to
a higher track, which heads south.

The track comes to a more prominent
forestry track by more game bird-rearing
pens. Almost immediately after take the left
fork track, which soon reaches and follows
the plantation's eastern perimeter with cow
pastures to the left and the conifer-wooded
valley dropping away to the right.

Through a gate at the top of the forest
the path comes to open hillside. More North
Berwyn Way signs guide the route up grassy
tracks. Take the first right fork to climb southwards on to Moel Fferna's lower slopes. The
lower field of grass and bracken is soon
replaced by heather and bilberry as a pleasant grassy path climbs towards the ridge.

At a clear junction (GR 123405) ignore the
way marker and take the right fork, which
climbs directly to Moel Fferna's summit.

Other route options

There are many options from Glyndyfrdwy,
including the tarred estate road that leaves
the A5 at GR 153427 and climbs to meet
Route B1 near the ridge and the road to Plas-
newydd in Cwm Uchaf – but they are inferior
to Route B1. By parking at the Ceiriog Forest
car park at GR 164382, 3 miles/5km west of
Glyn Ceiriog, you start high, but lose out on
some very pleasant scenery.

Alternative routes start from Cynwyd in the
Dee Valley south-west of Corwen and climb
east through the Cynwyd Forest. For those
who don't mind a long walk, Llangollen
makes a good start, again using North Berwyn Way routes along the enclosed bridleway track climbing west of Fron-Bache to
Ffynnon-las, where a track continues to Vivod
Mountain and onwards to Moel Fferna.

RIDGE ROUTES

Vivod Mountain

Distance: 3¾ miles/ 6km
Height gain: 410ft/125m
Time: 1½ hours

The ridge fence acts a guide all the way by a
rutted vehicle track across the heather. Soon
this follows the top edge of the Ceiriog Forest
and crosses a tarred lane. After a slight climb
to a subsidiary peak, it descends to the head
of the Ro Valley, a pleasant pastured hollow.
Beyond the forest, stay with the fence to go
left up the heather slopes of Vivod Mountain.

Cadair Bronwen

Distance: 4½ miles/ 7.3km
Height gain: 1210ft/370m
Time: 2½ hours

From the summit of Moel Fferna follow the peaty path down to a fence intersection. Over a ladder stile here head SSW alongside a fence. A peaty path has developed by the fence and leads over Cerrig Coediog before angling down right to the head of the valley of the upper Ceiriog.

The continuing path passes above a small conifer plantation before, at another fence intersection (GR 091369), heading south down to the Wayfarer Memorial, a plaque set in a crag, and the flinted track known as Ffordd Saeson (Englishman's Road). Legend has it that it was from here that the army of Henry II was repelled by Owain Gwynedd. A peaty path climbs over undulating crag-encrusted knolls before reaching Cadair Bronwen's rounded summit.

Right: On the summit of Moel Fferna.

Rising from the north Berwyn ridge like a great whale's back, Cadair Bronwen, the seat of the white breast, is the most northerly of the range's big three. Here the first of the broken crags which typify the Berwyn's eastern edge breaks through the surface, high above the head of Cwm Llawenog. Today a large cairn tops the summit, but the name Bwrdd Arthur on the OS Explorer map rekindles the legend that here was the site of King Arthur's Round Table. It would certainly have been quite an inhospitable place to hold one of their meetings.

Two ancient highways criss-cross the Berwyn ridge either side of Cadair Bronwen. To the south, linking Hendwr near Llandrillo with Llanrhaeadr ym Mochnant in the east, is Ffordd Gam Elin, Helen's winding road. This is believed to date back to the Roman occupation and is named after Helen, the wife of Emperor Maximus. To the north is Ffordd Saeson, the Englishman's Road.

Being further afield from the popular start points the mountain gets fewer visitors, but any omission of Cadair Bronwen would be an error of judgement as the remoteness lends it an eerie quietude. Looking north across vast heather tracts, which stretch almost as far as the eye can see above the valley of the Dee, only the patches of forestry dispel the aura of wilderness.

Opposite: Cadair Bronwen seen from the south-west.
Above: The Nant Rhydwilym track to the Wayfarer Memorial.

Route B3
Llanarmon DC and the Wayfarer Memorial

A very long route through heather moors
Start: Llanarmon Dyffryn Ceiriog
   (GR: SJ 157328)
Distance: 8½ miles (14km)
Height gain: 2165ft/660m
Time: 5 hours

From Llanarmon the quiet Ceiriog valley road is quickest and best, as the rights of way tend to be obstructed or slow going. The lane passes through the pastoral valley of the upper Ceiriog, with long cwms opening up to the left. The scenery gets wilder as the road ends beneath the rocks of Graig Fawr.

The Ceiriog valley slips away north beneath the rocks and the road becomes a stony track running alongside the south bank of Nant Rhydwilym. The track crosses a bridge over the stream before following the north bank through heather moorland. Beyond some conifer copses the track climbs to the pass of Bwlch Llandrillo, where there are a few crags and the Wayfarer Memorial Stone. This is dedicated to the influential cycling writer W. M. Robinson (1877–1956), who wrote under the name of 'Wayfarer' and was a lover of Wales.

A narrow peaty path climbs the rock-interspersed grassy ridge southwards, passing the head of Cwm Llawenog, a long and pleasant pastured valley. The crags of Cadair Berwyn, which overlook the cwm, have come into view by now and it's a short climb to the rounded grassy summit.

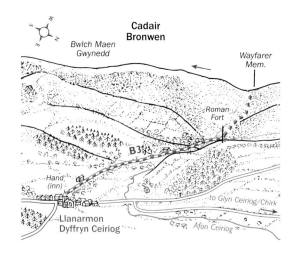

Route B4
Llidiart-cae-hir, Mynydd Tarw and Tomle
Splendid views on a very long approach to the main ridge

Start: Llidiart-cae-hir (roadside car parking) (GR: SJ 146309)

Distance: 6¼ miles (10km)

Height gain: 2100ft/640m

Time: 4 hours

At the road junction go over the step stile into the field. Head north-west to a gateway at the far side of the field. Through this gateway a boggy rush-infested track rounds the head of a pastured cwm. At the next gate leave the track and head WNW, climbing gradually across pastured hillside, soon to overlook the pleasant farming valley of the Gwrachen.

The best route (no path on the ground) stays a few paces to the north of Garnedd-wen's ridge – this way you'll find all the gates in the cross-fences. The aim now is to cross a saddle of land between the Gwrachen valley and Cwm Maen Gwynedd, a feat complicated by gates not being in quite the right places. After passing through a gate below a small cairn at the fence intersection at GR 135312, descend half-right towards a gate in a lower fence running parallel to the ridge (not shown on current maps).

Through the gate a clear path curves through rushy pastures to join the marked footpath at GR 130315. Go over a step stile here and follow the fence on the left. Beyond the next gate turn right and climb steep grass slopes to the unnamed summit (591m spot

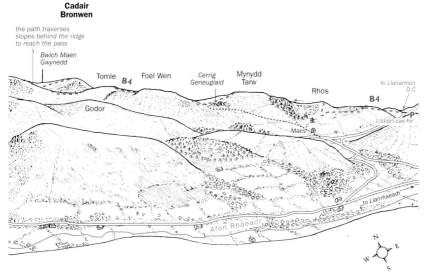

277

Above: Cadair Bronwen beyond the slopes of Tomle.

height) with the ancient tumulus on the top.

The views have widened and you can now see Moel Sych at the head of Cwm Maen Gwynedd. Follow a clear fence-side path along the grassy ridge, which curves left to the craggy Rhos. The low fence will have to be crossed as it approaches the conifers which cloak Mynydd Tarw's east flank. From here the vegetation changes to heather and bilberry and a path climbs above the forest to the large ancient cairn topping Mynydd Tarw.

This has been hollowed out to form a wind-shelter.

After passing the rugged cone-like rock tors of Cerrig Geneugiaid and rounding a rock-fringed cwm, the track continues westwards over Foel Wen and Tomle, where the crags of Cadair Berwyn become prominent. Just beneath them take the fine ledge-like path on the right to the pass of Bwlch Maen Gwynedd and on to Cadair Bronwen's summit.

Route B5
Cynwyd and the Wayfarer Memorial

A long western approach in the footsteps of
*   the drovers*

Start: Rhydyglafes (GR: SJ 049398)
Distance: 5¼ miles (8.5km)
Height gain: 2295ft/700m
Time: 3–3½ hours

Follow a narrow tarred lane past the farming complex of Rhydyglafes. After passing into the shade of the trees and beyond Cwm-isaf farm, the lane climbs pastured hillsides high above the wooded valley of the Afon Llynor. At Rhos-y-maerdy the road degenerates into a flinted track and is joined by an old green road from Cynwyd.

The walled track is tree-lined in places and traverses high pastures beneath the rounded hill of Moel yr Henfaes. By now the main Berwyn ridge stretches across the skyline. Stay with the main track as it crosses Nant Gwyn, where it veers left across a moorland spur. After being joined by an old track from Llandrillo you come to the main ridge at the Wayfarer Memorial Stone, dedicated to the cycling writer W. M. Robinson (1877–1956), who wrote under the name of 'Wayfarer'.

A narrow peaty path climbs the rock-interspersed grassy ridge southwards, passing the head of Cwm Llawenog, a long and pleasant pastured valley. The crags of Cadair Berwyn, which overlook the cwm, have come into view by now. Here there's a fork in paths: the left one traverses the eastern flanks beneath the crags, while the right one climbs the ridge above the crags to the rounded grassy summit.

Below: Descending to the Dee Valley from Cadair Berwyn.

Route B6
Moel Ty-uchaf and the Stone Circle

Another ancient route visiting a fine stone circle

Start: Llandrillo (GR: SJ 035371)
Distance: 4 miles (6.5km)
Height gain: 2080ft/635m
Time: 2½ hours

From the riverside car park turn left along the main road before taking the right fork by the war memorial. Go straight on at the next junction, following the lane uphill to its terminus. Ignore the farm drive on the left but carry on towards the woods ahead. A rough track now angles left passing the cottage of Ty'n-y-cae-mawr. The track heads north-east,

gradually veering eastwards among rough pastures, often with woodland below.

On reaching a crossroads of tracks, turn right on the slopes of Moel Ty-uchaf. Detour left before the woods of Coed Gerynant to see the fine Bronze Age stone circle, which is around 10 yards/m in diameter and consists of 43 stones with a cist in the centre.

Aim for the bottom right-hand corner of the forest to return to the track at its terminus. Through a gate at the end of the track a path continues the climb up the grass slopes of Moel Pearce. Where the path veers right towards Bwlch Maen Gwynedd leave it to stay by the fence, which climbs to Cadair Bronwen's summit.

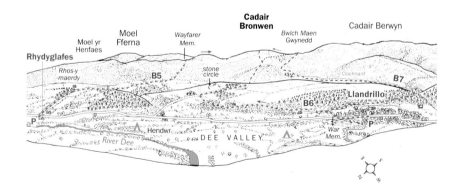

Above: The stone circle of Moel Ty-uchaf.

Route B7
Llandrillo and Clochnant
A wild but direct approach
Start: Llandrillo (GR: SJ 035371)
Distance: 4¼ miles (6.8km)
Height gain: 2065ft/630m
Time: 2½ hours

From the riverside car park turn left along the main road. Take the right fork by the war memorial, then the narrow tarred country lane on the right. This ends at Lechwedd Farm, but a good track continues uphill to the lower edge of the forest. The grassy track eventually enters the forest. Take the left fork at the next junction to emerge on open moorland.

The track runs parallel to the Clochnant stream and becomes very faint and marshy. Ignore the path crossing the stream but continue up the cwm. The going improves as it crosses terrain cloaked with heather and bracken. After passing a small conifer copse the path climbs to Bwlch Maen Gwynedd where you climb north along the ridge to Cadair Bronwyn.

Descent
The key to the descent is to take the left fork track just below the summit of the Bwlch Maen Gwynedd pass and to descend to the valley bottom, rather than heading towards the Moel Pearce ridge. The track is joined by a rougher track descending Blaen Trawsnant and heads for a block of pine trees with the Clochnant stream below to the left. The track fades as it traverses a tract of rushy ground but becomes more prominent again as it approaches the forests of Cwm Pennant. On reaching a fork in the tracks take the right one, which descends to Lechwedd Farm. Here lanes lead back to Llandrillo.

Other route options
No direct access from Cwm Llawenog means that most alternatives would be contrived. A route from Cwm Maen Gwynedd by way of Mynydd Tarw and Tomle is feasible, using the path that traverses the north slopes of Cadair Berwyn. Thick heather means that slopes with no paths would be tortuous and impractical.

Opposite: Cwm Clochnant, Berwyns.

RIDGE ROUTES

Moel Fferna
Distance: 4½ miles/7.3km
Height gain: 690ft/210m
Time: 2 hours

An undulating path alongside the ridge-fence leads over a couple of rock-crusted knolls down to Ffordd Saeson and the Wayfarer Memorial plaque before climbing north, then north-east, still alongside a ridge fence. At the fence intersection at GR 111380 turn left (NNW) to climb the crag-fringed heather knoll of Cerrig Coedog where a peaty path continues to Moel Fferna.

Cadair Berwyn
Distance: 1½ miles/2.4km
Height gain: 390ft/120m
Time: 1 hour

The ridge fence acts as a guide all the way, firstly on the downward slopes to the pass marked as Bwlch Maen Gwynedd on current maps, then on the steep climb to the unnamed peak north of Cadair Berwyn. Now much easier going, the clear ridge path continues to Cadair Berwyn's north top before climbing to the rocky tor of the higher south top.

This Berwyn centrepiece isn't content with one peak, it has two; you could even say three if you count the un-named rise above Blaen–cwm-llawenog (spot height 794m). The cairned north top (827m), standing proud above the long valley of Cwm Maen Gwynedd, is more rounded, but the south top is an angular craggy tor, the culmination of the Godor ridge to the east, and fittingly spectacular for the highest summit in the range.

Cadair Berwyn's east face is fronted by crag, not the kind climbers would flock to but an attractive fringe of fractured cliffs that catches the light and adds texture to match the tweedy colours of the heather, moor grasses and bracken. Cwm Lluncaws to the south of the summit is beautifully sculpted and, although its lake clings more closely to the sides of neighbouring Moel Sych, most views of it include Cadair Berwyn's pyrami-dal southern crags. In the west the slopes are of grass and heather and fall in three long spurs to the Dee Valley.

The most popular approaches by far are those from Tan-y-pistyll. There's good reason for the popularity. Before you start you're confronted by the spectacular waterfalls of Pistyll Rhaeadr, and there's a fine walk though glacial cwms and rocky edges all the way to the ridge. In contrast, climbs from the west are long, rambling, more moorland in nature, and contain no hint of the mountain drama to come. But that's the Berwyn for you: secretive to the last.

Opposite: Moel Sych and Cadair Berwyn.
Above: The South Top of Cadair Berwyn .

Route B8
Tyn-y-ffridd and Blaen y Cwm
Follow old quarry tracks
Start: Tyn-y-ffridd (GR: SJ 117308). Limited
 car parking (GR: SJ 119306) by the bridge
 over Afon Twrch
Distance: 4¼ miles/7.5km
Height gain: 1870ft/570m
Time: 2½ hours

From the roadside parking at the bridge climb
the narrow lane back to Tyn-y-ffridd before
turning left along the lane through the
verdant valley of Cwm Maen Gwynedd. At
the road-end continue in the same direction

along a farm track passing Blaen y Cwm and
a couple of small forestry plantations. The
hills close in and the view is overwhelmed by
the steep slopes and crags of Cadair Berwyn
at the head of the cwm.

At GR 084327 leave the track for a grass
path raking up hillslopes to the right, and
aiming for a narrow col between Cadair
Berwyn and the rounded moorland top of
Tomle.

Go through a gate on reaching the col. If
you're a bagger of 2000ft peaks you'll want to
detour right to Tomle first, but two options
await you to achieve the summit of Cadair
Berwyn. The easier one cuts across the north-

Opposite: Looking across Tomle to Cadair Berwyn.

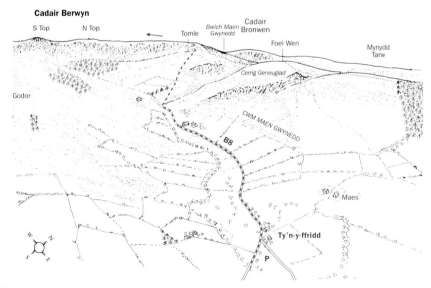

ern face of Cadair Berwyn, high above Cwm Llawenog to reach Bwlch Maen Gwynedd, where a steady grass and peat ridge leads south to the northern summit. The second option is the steep, rugged path which climbs directly to the north summit. The ridge path continues from the north summit to the higher and craggier south summit.

Descent

Head north past the north top trig point to the fence corner at GR 076336, where a grassy rake leads down to the col beneath Tomle. Now a ridge fence leads over the ridge to Rhos, passing over Tomle and the twin summits of Foel Wen before reaching Mynydd Tarw's wind shelter.

Continue along the upper perimeter of the forest to the grass and crag ridge of Rhos before rounding the cwm on the right to the grassy peak (591m spot height on Explorer maps). On reaching the tumulus on the summit follow the fence down to a gate at GR 123314. Turn left through this and follow the fence on the right to the next step stile in a cross-fence. Just beyond this you'll see a tractor track through rushes arcing right to another gate.

Through this gate, rake across the grassy Garneddwen ridge's northern slopes. Keep just below the ridge to locate the gates in the fences. Eventually you come to an ill-defined rushy track which rounds a small grassy cwm. Go right along this to reach the lane at Llidiart-cae-hir.

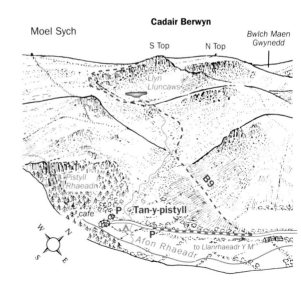

Opposite: Walking on the Nant y Llyn path to Moel Sych.

Route B9
Tan-y-pistyll and Llyn Lluncaws
The classic waterfall route
Start: Roadside lay-by parking 200m short of
  Tan-y-pistyll farm/café (GR: SJ 076293)
Distance: 3 miles/5km
Height gain: 1900ft/580m
Time: 1½ hours

Tan-y-Pistyll is a spectacular place with oak
woods, craggy hillsides and, at the head of
the valley, the tree-hung cliffs down which
the 200ft/60m Pistyll Rhaeadr foams. You
could decide to park yourself on the café
terrace with a cool drink and stay all day. It
would be a wise move, too. But the Berwyn
Mountains are waiting. The highest are just
out of view at present, but they'll soon reveal
themselves.

From the roadside car park south-east of
the farm/café complex turn right along the
road in the Llanrhaeadr ym Mochnant direction. After about 400 yards/m, go through a
farm gate on the left to follow a wide grassy
track into the cwm of Nant y Llyn. The cliffs of
Moel Sych and Cadair Berwyn now form a
fine spectacle at the head of the cwm.

The track degenerates into a path, which
fords two streams before coming to Llyn
Lluncaws, a fine tarn surrounded by tussocky
grass and heather. Those cliffs are now seen
to full vantage.

A peaty path climbs south of the lake and
up a grassy spur to the base of Moel Sych's
crags. Follow the path along the edge of the
crags to reach the col between Moel Sych
and Cadair Berwyn, before climbing to the
rocky south top of the latter peak.

Route B10
Llandrillo and Bwlch Maen Gwynedd

A wild but direct approach to the highest summit

Start: Riverside car park, Llandrillo
(GR: SJ 035371)

Distance: 4¾ miles/7.6km

Height gain: 2265ft/690m

Time: 3 hours

From the small riverside car park in the village, turn left along the main road towards Corwen. After taking the right fork street by the war memorial, turn right along a narrow tarred country lane, which ends at Lechwedd Farm. A good track continues uphill to the lower edge of the forest covering the slopes of Cefn Pen-llety. The grassy track eventually enters the forest.

Take the left fork at the next junction to emerge on wild open hillside. The track runs parallel to the Clochnant stream and becomes very faint and marshy. Ignore the path crossing the stream but continue up the cwm. The going improves as it crosses terrain cloaked with heather and bracken.

After passing a small conifer copse the path continues over streamside slopes of heather and grass before climbing to the wild pass marked on the map as Bwlch Maen Gwynedd. Ignore the path traversing the craggy northern slopes at the head of Cwm Llawenog. Instead, climb on the main ridge path to an unnamed subsidiary peak before continuing south to Cadair Berwyn's two summits.

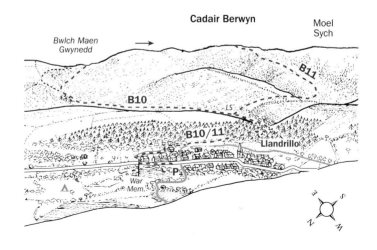

Above: Looking down Cwm Maen Gwynedd to Moel Sych (left) and Cadair Berwyn (right).

Descent

Head north by the ridge fence, passing the trig point and cairn of the north top and following the fence around the northern cliffs down to the north-western side of the Bwlch Maen Gwynedd pass beneath Cadair Bronwen. The key to the descent is to take the left fork track just west of the summit of the Bwlch Maen Gwynedd pass and to descend to the valley bottom rather than heading towards the Moel Pearce ridge.

The track is joined by a rougher track descending Blaen Trawsnant and heads for a block of pine trees with the Clochnant stream below left. The track fades as it traverses a tract of rushy ground but becomes more prominent again as it approaches the forests of Cwm Pennant. On reaching a fork in the tracks take the right one, which descends to Lechwedd Farm. Here lanes lead back to Llandrillo.

Route B11
Llandrillo and Foel Fawr

A wild but direct approach to the highest
*   summit*

Start: Riverside car park, Llandrillo
    (GR: SJ 035371)
Distance: 4½ miles/7.2km
Height gain: 2400ft/730m
Time: 2½–3 hours

As in Route B10, turn left along the main road through the village, take the right fork by the war memorial and the narrow tarred country lane on the right to Lechwedd Farm. Continue on the good track, which passes beneath then enters the forest covering the slopes of Cefn Pen-llety. Take the left fork at the next junction to emerge on wild open hillside.

The track heads eastwards parallel to the Clochnant stream to GR 047352, where you'll see a ladder stile beyond the river crossing. Over the stile a faint path, marked with the odd white arrow, stays close to a wall (later a fence) on the left. After going over another ladder stile in a cross-fence the path fords Nant Cwm Tywyll and climbs to a cairn on the low shoulder of Foel Fawr's grassy spur. Now you swing left uphill.

The path is faint at first but becomes more prominent beyond a ladder stile until just before the summit where it fades away. Maintain direction to reach the trig point on the north summit, and then head south for the rocky and higher south summit.

Descent

From the south summit head north to the trig point on the north summit before descending WNW across the upper grass slopes. A path soon develops and descends down the ridge of Foel Fawr. Lower down the path fades but a ladder stile in a fence at the far side of the Nant Cwm Tywyll stream to your right is the key to the concessionary path marked with orange dashes on the OS Explorer map.

Follow this northwards to another ladder stile in a cross fence. Beyond this a fence on the right acts as a guide to the Clochnant stream, which lies beyond another ladder stile. After crossing the stream climb the far banks to a track that leads westwards towards the forests of Cwm Pennant. Take the right fork track, which descends through, then below, the forests to Lechwedd Farm, where lanes lead back to Llandrillo.

Other route options

A good option would be to follow Route B14 to Mynydd Tarw from Tyn-y-fridd. This climbs on the farm lane past Maes before climbing pastures towards the bottom left end of a conifer plantation cloaking the east flank of Mynydd Tarw. The track becomes clearer beyond an old gatepost and rakes across the south slopes of Tarw and underneath the crags of Cerrig Geneugiaid to reach the ridge.

A fence guides the route over the ridges of Foel Wen and Tomle to the col beneath the craggy nose of Cadair Berwyn's northern end. Climb the nose to gain the ridge.

RIDGE ROUTES

Cadair Bronwen

Distance: 1½ miles/2.4km
Height gain: 295ft/90m
Time: ¼ hour

From the south top follow the ridge fence past the cairn and trig point of the north top, over the unnamed summit, down to the col between Cwm Llawenog and Cwm Clochnant, then climb the easy slopes to Cadair Bronwen's summit. It's easy and has fine views over the edge into several moorland cwms.

Godor

Distance: 2 miles/3.3km
Height gain: 260ft/80m
Time: 1 hour

Note: not suitable for wintry conditions when a snow cornice and ice on the narrow path might well make this route unsafe.

From the south top descend south towards Moel Sych. Just before the col between the two watch out for a path that slants down a gulley back towards a fence corner beneath the cliffs. On reaching the fence, follow it down on grass towards the subsidiary summit of Moel yr Ewig and continue above the conifers of Cwm Maen Gwynedd's southern slopes. Be careful in mist not to be enticed too far on to a southern spur by the fence.

Where it changes direction leave it to head south-east across an increasingly rough ridge towards Godor. The tussocks get more vicious with every step as you approach the 675m west top, but things improve as you reach the highest summit.

Note: there are no legal routes off Godor and for this reason I have not included the mountain as a separate entity.

Moel Sych

Distance: ½ mile/800m
Height gain: 130ft/40m
Time: 15–20 minutes

A short and simple stroll, either by the ridge fence which goes all the way to Moel Sych's summit, or by the edge path. This hugs the top of the crags surrounding Llyn Lluncaws before climbing half-right back to the ridge fence and summit.

Moel Sych, the dry hill, seems a misnomer if you've tackled it from the high road at Milltir Gerrig, for this, the most southerly peak of the Central Berwyn ridge, has real connections with water. This approach is the wettest in the region: Wales's highest and most spectacular waterfall, Pistyll Rhaeadr, lies not 3 miles/5km away, and Moel Sych is the only peak to have its very own corrie lake, Llyn Lluncaws.

Opposite: Moel Sych across Afon Disgynfa.
Below: On the summit of Moel Sych.

Once considered as being the highest Berwyn, Moel Sych is now just the big rounded one on the end. However, it has a powerful presence and, like its neighbours, is enhanced with crags on the eastern edge. Besides the previously mentioned west ridge to Milltir Gerrig, Moel Sych throws out a rather bulbous south ridge, which declines to the wild hanging valley of the Afon Disgynfa, the stream feeding Pistyll Rhaeadr.

Deep within this valley lies Rhos y Beddau, a 36ft/11m diameter Bronze Age stone circle with a 200ft/60m long row of standing stones leading up to it. Often in summer it's hard to appreciate the stones, for the vegetation of rushes and heather is prolific – historians are best advised to visit outside the summer months.

Route B12

Tan-y-pistyll and the South Ridge

A bit of a grind, but a good descent route
with a view over the waterfalls

Start: Roadside lay-by parking 200m short of
Tan-y-pistyll farm/café (GR: SJ 076293)

Distance: 3 miles/5km

Height gain: 1900ft/580m

Time: 2 hours

Turn left up the road to Tan-y-pistyll, towards the Pistyll Rhaeadr waterfalls at the head of the lower valley. On reaching the farmhouse/café and its car park, it's well worth detouring left past the toilet block and information sign to see the magnificent falls tumbling to the deep pool beneath the cliffs.

Back at the car park follow the wide path of the main route, through a gate just beyond the toilet block. It skirts the bottom of the wooded hillslopes. Beyond the woods take the left fork path climbing to a higher flinted track, where you climb left to reach the hanging valley at the top of the falls (which is a short detour left).

Ignore paths delving deeper into the cwm of the Afon Disgynfa and instead climb right on a clear path winding up grassy slopes with fine retrospective views of the valley. Soon the path climbs up the spur of Trum Felen staying by the fence all the way to Moel Sych's summit.

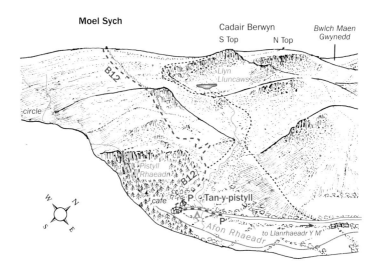

Above: Llyn Lluncaws.

Route B13

Milltir Cerrig and the West Ridge

High start; rough soggy trek eased by an engineered path

Start: Old quarry at Milltir Gerrig
(GR: SJ 017305)

Distance: 3¼ miles/6km

Height gain: 1180ft/360m

Time: 2–2½ hours

The car park is on an old quarry and its access track by the Powys/Merionydd border sign. The walk proper starts just north on an old unsurfaced road descending to Llandrillo, but rather than following the road to it, take a faint path heading south-west then south across grassland. It meets the old highway by a notice-board at its junction with the Berwyn ridge path (GR 018303).

Take the right fork, which leads west up the long, long ridge. Soon you'll encounter duckboards and railway sleepers, which have been laid across the peaty marshes. The green pastures and low fertile foothills of the distant Dee Valley contrast with the starkness of the surrounding moor.

On reaching a cairned heather knoll, Craig Wen, you'll see the wild moorland hollow of the Afon Disgynfa sneaking away to the right. It's hard to believe that not two miles away children will be eating ice creams or tucking into steak pie and chips at Tan-y-pistyll, the café beneath the Pistyll Rhaeadr waterfalls. The main Berwyn ridge stretches across the horizon but Moel Sych itself hides behind the domed heather slopes of Cerrig Duon. It's one of those mountains with many false summits. Even from the wind shelter (marked cairn) at GR 041309 it hides itself from view.

Moel Sych's summit finally comes into view beyond Cerrig Duon, and is highlighted by the fence that climbs straight up the middle to its summit. The summit itself is a plain affair with a cairn and two ladder stiles in intersecting fences.

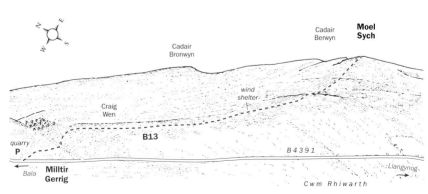

Above: High on Moel Sych's west ridge.

Other route options

The obvious one is to use the Route B16 path to the top of the falls as far as the stream, Nant y Cerrig-duon, before climbing north on a faint path up Cwm Rhiwiau. There's some very rough terrain to cross in the upper reaches, where an intermittent path leads to the south ridge, just below its steep final climb to the summit.

To complete a Llandrillo circuit without doing the whole of the west ridge, you could descend from the wind shelter at GR 041309 north along the moorland spur of Yr Aran to meet a track at GR 032333. This concessionary Tir Gofal route descends to the hamlet of Pennant, where a tarred lane leads back to Llandrillo.

RIDGE ROUTE

Cadair Berwyn

Distance: ½ mile/ 800m
Height gain: 130ft/40m
Time: 15–20 minutes

The ridge fence/wall acts as a guide all the way. As the path nears the cliff-edge it is joined by one which has climbed up the east spur from Llyn Lluncaws. The path now climbs to the rocky south top of Cadair Berwyn.

Mynydd Tarw, the bull mountain, lies in the middle of a long eastern ridge thrown out by Cadair Berwyn. On the south-facing Cwm Maen Gwynedd side its steep flank has been tamed by high pastures and a spread of conifers which stretches right to the summit. On the south side, wilder heather and moor grass slopes decline to Cwm-y-geifr.

The most notable features of the mountain are the outcropping crags known as Cerrig Geneugiaid, which protrude almost unnaturally from the ridge to the north of the summit. The summit itself has a Neolithic cairn, which has been hollowed out to form a wind shelter. Views from the summit are good, with the high Berwyn ridge filling most of the western skyline, while waves of rolling hillside to the north and east fade to the hazy outlines of the hills of Shropshire and Cheshire.

Opposite: The ancient cairn on the summit of Mynydd Tarw.

Route B14
Tyn-y-ffridd and Cerrig Geneugiaid
A short but pleasant route with fine views
Start: Tyn-y-ffridd (GR: SJ 117308). Limited car parking (GR: SJ 119306) by the bridge over Afon Twrch
Distance: 2¼ miles/3.7km
Height gain: 1230ft/375m
Time: 1½ hours

From the bridge at Tyn-y-ffridd climb along the road back to the junction at Tyn-y-ffridd, where you turn left then immediately right by the telephone box. The lane passes through a farming complex before climbing past a second farm at Maes.

Where the lane veers right towards Fotty (Votty on maps) leave it to fork left on a faint track to the right of a hedge climbing NNW across a field to a gate at the far end. Now turn right and follow the fence. At the field corner you join a good track climbing towards the bottom end of a conifer plantation. The track is faint to non-existent as you turn left on reaching the conifers, but you'll pick it up at the top left end of the high field.

Soon you leave the pastures for the high moor as the route rakes across the south slopes of Tarw. The views down the valley of Cwm Maen Gwynedd now include Moel Sych and the high Berwyn ridge, although the slopes of Tomle partially block out the crags of Cadair Berwyn. After tucking underneath the impressive conical crags of Cerrig Geneu-giaid, the track comes to the ridge.

After passing the top edge of the crags, follow the peaty fence-side path eastwards through heathery terrain to the large wind-shelter on Mynydd Tarw's summit.

Other route options

You could start at Llidiart-cae-hir and follow Route B4, or an even longer route from Llan-armon Dyffryn Ceiriog using footpaths on the south side of Nant Maengwyn.

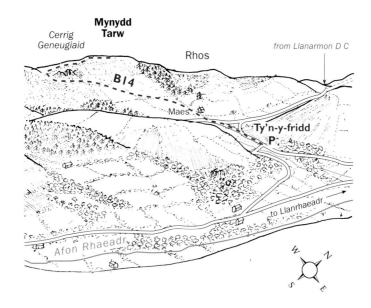

RIDGE ROUTES

Cadair Berwyn
Distance: 3½ miles/5.6km
Height gain: 1015ft/310m
Time: 2 hours

Descend westwards, keeping the cone-like rock tors of Cerrig Geneugiaid to the left. The path is clear enough all the way and follows the fence across heathery terrain, over the twin humps of Foel Wen, where a long but steady ascent of Tomle begins.

Once over Tomle there's a slight descent to a four-way junction of paths beneath the nose of Cadair Berwyn's northern end. Take the bold grassy route up the nose before turning left along the craggy rim of the ridge or, if snow cornices have formed along this edge, the clear path higher up. Both routes visit the north top and its trig point before continuing to the rocky south top.

Rhos
Distance: 1mile/1.5km
Height gain: 50ft/15m
Time: ½ hour

Head north-east along the top edge of the forest cloaking Mynydd Tarw's western flanks. Beyond the forest the terrain changes from heather to grass. Continue alongside the fence to the crags which top the summit of Rhos. The rounded summit to the south (591m spot height) is worth the detour for it is topped by an ancient burial tomb.

Below: On Mynydd Tarw's east ridge looking into Cwm Maen Gwynedd.

POST GWYN

On a remote ridge between the Llangynog–Bala road in Cwm Rhiwarth and the sullen and uninhabited cwm of Afon Disgynfa, Post Gwyn, the white post, is a rather awkward-to-get-to outlier of the high Berwyn. Heather predominates, especially in the north where its ridge branches off from Moel Sych's western arm. The little summit, however, is blessed with a few crags set among grass and a smattering of heather and is an extremely pleasant place to be.

Many walkers approach the peak from the high pass of Milltir Gerrig on the Llangynog–Bala road but they will find the route to be tiresome and unrewarding outside the driest of summer months, for the terrain is of deep heather, marshy peat and cotton grass. The way to tackle Post Gwyn is from the east, probably combining it with a circuit of Moel Sych and Cadair Berwyn.

Left: The summit cairn of Post Gwyn.

Route B15
Llangynog and the east ridge

A route of contrasts, lush green fields, craggy
*   peaks and sullen wild moor*

Start: Roadside lay-by parking 200m short of
    Tan-y-pistyll farm/café (GR: SJ 076293)
Distance: 2½ miles/4km
Height gain: 1346ft/410m
Time: 1½ hours

From the roadside lay-by in Pencraig, climb
the hill to the first gate beside the forest in
Cwm Orog. A slaty track continues uphill
with a stream to the left. Note that the track
doesn't stick to the right of way marked on
the map but is the way the landowners want
you to use. Take the right fork to pass an area
with a lock-up.

The right of way goes directly uphill
through a gap in the trees here, but the footpath sign points to the right along another
slaty track. It exits the forest at GR 053277,
some way south of the marked path. Continue along the track through access land to
round the head of Cwm Glan-hafon on to the
Post Gwyn ridge.

At a gate just short of another forest leave
the track and turn left along the ridge, where
a faint track leads to a gate at the south west
corner of the same plantation. Go through
this and continue along the ridge following a
narrow path. The path all but fades out by
several shallow pools but by keeping just
right of the last one you should be able to
pick out a faint sheep-track of a path which
keeps slightly right of the highest ground.

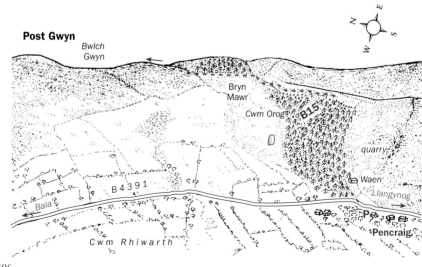

Above: Nearing the summit of Post Gwyn.

By now Post Gwyn's summit cairn shows itself clearly ahead. A fence, not shown on the map, straddles the ridge. There's no stile as yet but it's low and quite easy to hop over. The path disappears again but by aiming for the slightly higher and green patch half-left, you'll be able to pick up another faint sheep-trod, which eventually arcs slightly left before climbing to the summit.

Route B16
Pistyll Rhaeadr and Afon Disgynfa

Waterfalls and ancient circles: a walk back in time

Start: B4391, Pencraig, Llangynog
  (GR: SJ 046274)

Distance: 2½ miles/4km

Height gain: 1410ft/430m

Time: 1½–2 hours

Follow the lane towards Tan-y-pistyll at the head of the valley and turn right by the car park to follow a wide path through a gate just beyond the toilet block. This skirts the bottom of the wooded hillslopes to the north of Pistyll Rhaeadr waterfalls. Beyond the woods take the left fork path climbing to a higher flinted track, where you climb left to reach the hanging valley at the top of the falls, which can be seen by a short detour to the left.

This route continues up the valley of the Disgynfa and ignores the more prominent path on the right climbing Moel Sych's south ridge.

The path fades a little on nearing Cwm Rhi-wiau. Among the rushes you may be able to seek out the cairn and stone circle. Cross the stream and follow the now easier south bank to locate a shepherds' path climbing south then SSW on the right side of the hollow of Cwm Llwyd-mawr. Leave this track as it levels out on the ridge for a narrow sheep track climbing Post Gwyn's easy grass slopes to reach the summit cairn.

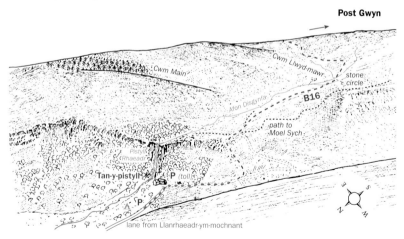

Opposite: Pistyll Rhaeadr at the start of Route B16.

Other route options

A rough route begins at Milltir Gerrig at the top of the Llangynog–Bala road and follows Route B13 across duckboards to the cairns on Lechwedd Groes, where you'll see the upper valley of Afon Disgynfa. Leave the main ridge path here to climb ESE along a rough, undefined ridge of heather, cotton grass and miry peat. The slog eventually leads to the summit, the second of two knolls.

RIDGE ROUTES

Mynydd Glan-hafon

Distance: 2½ miles/4km
Height gain: 330ft/100m
Time: 1–1¼ hours

Faint winding paths lead the route along the broad ridge. After crossing a fence straddling the ridge you'll come across some shallow pools. Head for the top right-hand corner of the forest ahead and go through a gate. Now there's a fence on your left to act as a guide.

After crossing a broad track, the route maintains direction on wheel-tracks in the grass to a gate at GR 067279. The path, now with a fence on the right, straddles Y Clogydd before coming to another gate at a path intersection. Now climb south-east (pathless, but gradually angling towards a fence on the left). You'll round the head of the narrow gorge of Nant Ddial to a fence intersection. Now the going is easy: follow a fence on your left to the summit of Mynydd Glan-hafon.

Craig Rhiwarth

Distance: 2 miles/3.2km
Height gain: 260ft/80m
Time: 1 hour

The section to the broad track crossing the ridge by the forest at GR 062285 is similar to the ridge route to Mynydd Glan-hafon. This time, though, turn right along the track and follow it to the entrance to the forest of Cwm Orog (GR 055276). (This track is not shown on current maps, at the time of writing in 2010.) Go through a gate on the left and follow a path alongside the forest's edge before angling left across the rushy field to the far fence. Go across this and continue alongside a fence dividing rough moor and a triangular lush green pasture. Angle right on a sunken track tackling the northern slopes of Craig Rhiwarth. It passes through the ancient ramparts of the Bronze Age fort. Now head south for the summit.

CRAIG RHIWARTH

Craig Rhiwarth rises defiantly in precipitous slopes of crag, scree, oak and birch scrub woodland and bracken. The remnants of past lead mining are there but don't detract from its majestic grandeur. Below it is Llangynog, the last outpost of the Tanat Valley, whose verdant fields are replaced by the windswept Berwyn moorland at Milltir Gerrig.

The summit of Craig Rhiwarth is almost completely filled by the hill fort of the same name, occupied from Bronze Age times well into the occupation by the Romans. The fort was bound on the north side by a stone rampart, but the precipitous nature of the hillside made it unnecessary to build any artificial defences on the other three sides. Inside the fort is a Bronze Age cairn and evidence of scores of circular structures.

Exciting as they may be, the slopes above Llangynog are too loose and steep to facilitate walking routes, which tend to go around the easier slopes of the north or start from higher up the Bala road.

Opposite: Craig Rhiwarth above the houses of Llangynog.
Above: Craig Rhiwarth summit looking to Mynydd Glan-hafon.

Route B17
Cwm Orog Mines

The quickest and most direct route to the summit

Start: B4391, Pencraig, Llangynog
(GR: SJ 046274) – roadside parking
Distance: ¾ mile/1.2km
Height gain: 900ft/275m
Time: ¾ hour

Climb the road before turning right along a stony drive passing some letterboxes. As the drive swings right towards the cottages at Waen, leave the track, which for a short distance is not in the access area, and continue alongside it on moorland to the right. Rejoin the track beyond the cottage for a short distance before taking a right turn on a slightly raised old miners' track. A little way further on take another right fork on a sunken grass track, which follows a fence uphill towards the Cwm Orog mines. The track is soon replaced by a narrow path continuing past some mine ruins and into a heather, bilberry and grass-covered hollow with Craig Rhiwarth's slopes to the right.

The route levels out and the path veers half-right to climb Rhiwarth's upper slopes to reach the small cairn crowning its highest top.

Descent

Head north from the summit to the north wall of the fort. Looking down you'll see a triangular, very green pasture just to the right of the conifers of Cwm Orog. You should also see a track leading down to the triangle's apex. Leave the track when you see a grassy hollow developing to the left with a narrow grassy spur to the right of it.

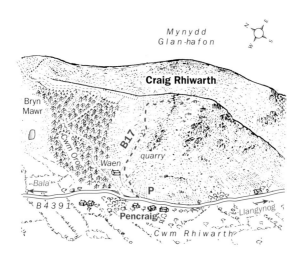

Go down the little spur, which descends beneath the heather and crag of Craig Rhiwarth's west ridge to the ruins of the Cwm Orog Mines. Continue downhill with a fence to your right. Stay on the moorland as the track from the cottages of Waun comes in from the right, but join it a short way downhill as it passes some letterboxes on the B4391 at Pencraig. (The reason for not joining the early part of the track from Waun is that it is not in access land.)

Below: Looking back from the Cwm Orog Mines to Cwm Rhiwarth.

Route B18

Cwm Glan-hafon

A more devious back-door route

Start: Llangynog village car park
(GR: SJ 053262)

Distance: 2 miles/3.2km

Height gain: 1245ft/380m

Time: 1½ hours

Turn right along the road passing over the bridge. Turn next right then right again to head east on the lane tucking beneath the rocky slopes of Craig Rhiwarth. Leave the lane for a splendid grass track on the left raking across Rhiwarth's low slopes. It passes through some oak woods before entering Cwm Glan-hafon, with the stream far below.

Ignore all tracks to the right and continue to the gap between Rhiwarth's north-east spur and Moel Crynddyn. Don't cross the stream but climb left along narrow trods through heather and bilberry – this can be rough and vegetation-choked during summer months. At Adwy'r Craig a cultivated green pasture appears to the right and the trods veer slightly left away from its edge to meet a track from the right. Turn left along this to cross the remains of the old fort's northern ramparts before continuing to the summit.

Other route options

A slightly longer but easier variant of Route B18 would be to cross the stream and continue up the left side of Cwm Glan-hafon past the sheepfolds. This is left of the right of way marked on the map. It climbs and zig-zags up slopes to the right before ending just north of Moel Crynddyn.

Now head west to a step stile in the fence at GR 058280 and maintain direction to reach a stony track. Follow this to the entrance of the Cwm Orog conifer planta-

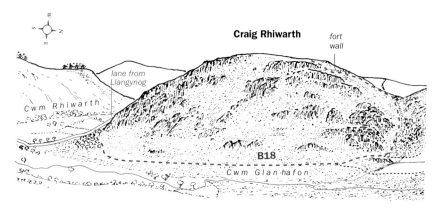

Craig Rhiwarth

fort wall

lane from Llangynog

Cwm Rhiwarth

B18

Cwm Glan-hafon

tions (GR 054276), but leave the track through a gate on the left. Head south across a rough field and cross the next fence on the left side of this field. You should now follow the fence – on the other side is a splendidly green and fertile triangular field.

By now you'll be able to pick out a track angling right up to the fringe of the hill. The rather artificial line you'll see hereabouts is the overgrown rampart of the old fort. The summit now lies to the south.

Above: Craig Rhiwarth from the north.

RIDGE ROUTE

Post Gwyn

Distance: 2 miles/3.2km
Height gain: 690ft/210m
Time: 1–1½ hours

Head north-westwards to pick up the track which angles half-right from the fort's northern ramparts, down towards the upper edge of the Cwm Orog spruce plantations. On reaching the apex of a triangular fertilised and green pasture, follow the fence along its north-western edge. Go over a cross-fence before making a diagonal to cross to the other side of a rushy field.

Follow the forest's edge and go through a gate to meet a flinted track coming out of the forest. Turn right along this track (not marked on current maps) and follow it towards a second plantation. On reaching its perimeter fence turn left to follow the Post Gwyn ridge to a second gate. Here the path gets less distinct. It fades completely beyond a couple of shallow pools but continue north-westwards on an open ridge, slightly wetter on the left side. After going over another cross-fence the path climbs the steeper slopes to Post Gwyn's summit.

MYNYDD GLAN-HAFON

Being next to Craig Rhiwarth has its disadvantages and Mynydd Glan-hafon (Glan-hafon on current maps) definitely suffers by comparison. It has crags, but they're aloof, and the farmers have been bold and tamed much more of the hillslopes into cow pastures scattered with hawthorn bushes. It's the sort of peak that if it had been in England would have been called White Hill.

The mountain is actually part of quite a long ridge separating the Tanat and Rhaeadr valleys. Indeed, on northern slopes you can make out the great falls of Pistyll Rhaeadr. It has two summits. The west one is at 608m, just a metre higher, and has crags, while the east summit has a trig point but no crag. From this second summit you can see the village of Llanrhaeadr-ym-Mochnant, which rather wonderfully means the blessed waterfall of the pig stream.

Like Craig Rhiwarth, Mynydd Glan-hafon has been mined for lead, zinc and copper and you pass a lead mine entrance on Route B19.

Left: Mynydd Glan-hafon from Llangynog.

Route B19
Llangynog and Cwm Glan-hafon

A fine route through the craggy Cwm Glan-hafon to an airy peak

Start: Llangynog village car park
(GR: SJ 053262)

Distance: 2¼ miles/4.5km

Height gain: 1475ft/450m

Time: 1¼ hours

From the village car park turn right and cross the bridge over the Afon Tanat. Turn right again through a gate on the far side of the bridge and follow the path along the north bank of the river. On reaching the last of three bridges head north (left) across fields to reach a lane at a sharp bend.

Turn right along the lane, then climb left on a tarred driveway passing some pretty cottages. This soon becomes a delightful grass track climbing into Cwm Glan-hafon, a deep pastoral hollow between the rugged slopes of Craig Rhiwarth (left) and Glan-hafon (right). Just beyond a stile and gate watch out for a right turn on a path which climbs with the Nant Ddial stream on the right. The path passes between former mines and soon begins some zig-zags beneath the crags and bracken fields of Y Clogydd.

As the path levels out leave it for a trackless course ESE to pass the rushy head of Nant Ddial and onwards to a vague ridge. Follow this towards Mynydd Glan-hafon, keeping the crags slightly to the right. A fence comes in from the left and leads to the summit area, again with the main crags to the right. The highest ground lies on the second of two prominent outcrops, although the trig point lies further north beyond a cross-fence.

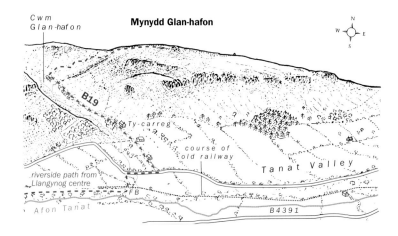

Other route options

An approach can be made from Tan-y-Pistyll crossing the stream beneath the Pistyll Rhaeadr waterfalls and following the zig-zagging mine tracks to the col between Y Clogydd (west) and Mynydd Glan-hafon. A south-easterly ascent, rough in places, takes the route around the head of Nant Ddial before climbing among the sparse crags to the summit.

Above right: A lead mine entrance at Cwm Glan-hafon.
Below: Mynydd Glan-hafon from Craig Rhiwarth. Route B19 climbs left of the stream to its head before aiming for the summit.

RIDGE ROUTE

Post Gwyn
Distance: 2½ miles/ 4km
Height gain: 525ft/160m
Time: 1–1½ hours

Follow the ridge fence WNW to a fence inter-section at the head of the rushy crag-lined gorge of Nant y Ddial, before descending on a pathless course north-eastwards to reach a gate at a path junction south-east of the knoll of Y Clogydd. Through the gate turn left to follow wheel-tracks keeping roughly parallel to the fence on your left. After going through another gate the ridge route continues towards a high forest.

On reaching the forest you cross a stony track and continue along the ridge, through another gate on to an open ridge with no guiding fence. Now indistinct, the route passes a couple of shallow pools. The driest ground is slightly on the north side of the ridge. Go over the next cross-fence and up on to Post Gwyn's pleasant summit.

Days Out: the Berwyn Mountains

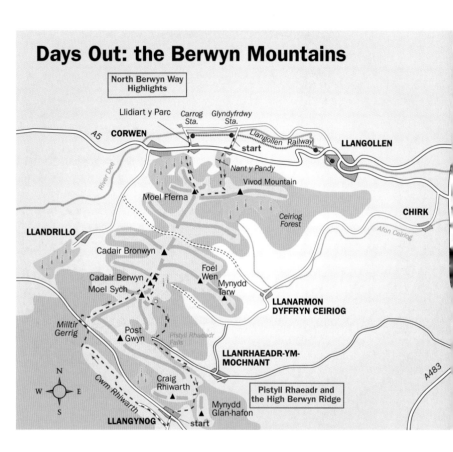

North Berwyn Way
Highlights

Llidiart y Parc

Carrog Sta.

Glyndyfrdwy Sta.

A5

CORWEN

Llangollen Railway

LLANGOLLEN

start

River Dee

Nant y Pandy

Vivod Mountain

CHIRK

Moel Fferna

Ceiriog Forest

Afon Ceiriog

LLANDRILLO

Cadair Bronwyn

Foel Wen

Cadair Berwyn
Moel Sych

Mynydd Tarw

LLANARMON
DYFFRYN CEIRIOG

Milltir Gerrig

Post Gwyn

Pistyll Rhaeadr Falls

LLANRHAEADR-YM-
MOCHNANT

A483

Cwm Rhiwarth

Craig Rhiwarth

Pistyll Rhaeadr and
the High Berwyn Ridge

N
W   E
S

Mynydd Glan-hafon

LLANGYNOG

start

Opposite: Striding on the Berwyn ridge.

Days Out: the Berwyn Mountains

Pistyll Rhaeadr and the High Berwyn Ridge

An entertaining mix of pastoral valleys and high ridges

Start: Llangynog (GR: SH 952300)

Distance: 13 miles (21km)

Height gain: 3050ft/930m

Time: 8 hours

From Llangynog's centre, follow the Cwm Pennant road, then turn right, following a narrow lane into Cwm Rhiwarth and along the western side of the river. This pleasant lane, lined by trees and hedgerow, hugs the foot of Hafod Hir's rock-fringed eastern slopes. At the road-end take the left fork, a flinted farm lane to Blaen-rhiwarth.

On reaching the farmhouse turn right along a rutted track that heads across fields to join a green road, which at one time would have been the main highway between Llangynog and Bala. It climbs parallel to the river and its more modern counterpart on the slaty slopes above and to the right. Soon the waterfalls at the head of the valley come into view, the white plume rustling in a tight, shaley ravine shaded by crag and slopes of bracken.

Beyond the falls and above a small copse

of larch and spruce, swing right on a track traversing moorland to reach the main Bala road at Milltir Gerrig (which means milestone). After turning left along the road for a short way, leave it for a track on the right, marked by a Berwyn Nature Reserve information board on the shoulder of the moor. Here the tracks divide.

Take the right fork which will head up the long heather and peat west ridge of the high Berwyn. Duckboards and railway sleepers help you negotiate some of the wetter parts of the ridge. After passing the cairns on Lechwedd Llwyd the route continues in a steady climb past a wind-shelter. Cadair Bronwen is the most prominent Berwyn at this stage as Moel Sych lies behind the rounded dome of Cerrig Duon. Eventually a fence-side path takes you up those final slopes to its broad, grassy summit.

Looking west from Moel Sych you can see the famous Snowdonian peaks spread along the horizon, from Cadair Idris, through the Rhinogs, then Snowdon and the distinctive Tryfan. This is a fine viewing platform even if it is an ordinary summit. Appearances however can be deceptive, and this is no ordinary moorland peak. Detour to the west a short way and you'll see the savage cliffs of the south side, Craig y Llyn, and a fine view down to the little blue tarn of Llyn Lluncaws.

Continue along the ridge to Cadair Berwyn's nearer and more southerly rocky top. It has now been discovered that this more southerly top is, at 830m, the highest of the whole group – 3m higher than the more rounded official summit which has the trig point on top. That's a boring place to eat your sandwiches anyway – it's much better to find a niche here in the rocks.

You could bag Cadair Bronwen, where it is said King Arthur had his round table, but it is little more than a rounded, grassy lump and has no new views – and not a table in sight. It would be better to head back. If Henry II had taken that advice when he came here eight hundred years ago, he wouldn't have had his army defeated so badly by the forces of Owain Gwynedd, then Prince of North Wales.

After retracing the route to Moel Sych's clifftops, the route descends on a grassy spur to the south of Llyn Lluncaws and crosses its outflow, Nant-y-llyn, before continuing on the slopes of bracken and boulders. It comes out to the little road through the Rhaeadr Valley at GR 079291.

By now you will have heard the thunderous roar of Wales's grandest waterfall, Pistyll Rhaeadr, and it's just a short way north-west up the road. Beyond Tan-y-pistyll farm you will see its waters plummeting over 200 feet/60 metres down sheer, tree-lined cliffs. Standing on the little footbridge at the base of the falls you cannot fail to be impressed by their sheer size and the volume of the foaming torrents.

Opposite: The ridge to Cadair Berwyn's south top.

Above: Pistyll Rhaeadr.

Cross the small bridge at the foot of the waterfalls and follow the waymarked path south-east down the valley to some old quarry workings. From the old quarry, you can either follow the quarry track as it zigzags out of the valley or continue to follow the yellow arrows on a strenuous but more direct route up the same slopes. This is the bridleway marked on the maps. The path, now a ribbon of grass through the bracken, climbs over high, windswept moorland between Y Clogydd and Mynydd Glan-hafon. Look back for a fine view to the main Berwyn cliffs.

Once across the moorland pass, the path descends south-westwards into a deep cwm between bracken-clad, rounded hills. Further down, its course meanders close to the stream. Be careful not to be led astray by a well-defined track beneath the crags of Y Clogydd. At GR 065274, by some hawthorn bushes and old slag heaps, the path meets a farm track, which should be followed south for about 400 yards/m before bearing right on a path that crosses the stream, Nant Sebon.

It climbs to meet another track beneath the rocky slopes of Craig Rhiwarth at a crossroads of routes. Ignore the track and instead maintain direction on a bridleway which eventually swings right, threading through some attractive woodland, still beneath fine scenery of crag and boulders. Llangynog appears through the trees and the bridleway meets a lane. The quiet lane takes half a mile to get there, skirting en route the foot of Craig Rhiwarth, with the green fields of the Tanat Valley on the other side.

North Berwyn Way Highlights

A stimulating walk to Moel Fferna, the
Berwyn Mountains' most northerly
2000ft peak

Start: Glyndyfrdwy (GR: SJ 148427)

Distance: 10 miles/16km (without using the
Llangollen Railway, which reduces it to
7½ miles/11.4km)

Height gain: 1670ft/510m

Time: 5½ hours

The Dee Valley west of Llangollen is one of the loveliest in Wales. It's not rugged with ice-sculpted rock mountains, but it is velvety smooth, green with field, hedgerow and woods tinged with the purple of heather moors. And then there's that beautiful, wildly meandering river.

The route begins in the village of Glyndyfrdwy, the home-place of Owain Glyndwr, that great warrior Prince of Wales, whose troops made forays into the Berwyn Mountains to conquer the English king, Henry IV.

The steam trains of the Llangollen railway run all year, and if you plan your journey right, you can begin or end it in 1950s fashion from Carrog, near Llidiart y Parc to Glyndyfrdwy. There's also a splendid country pub, the Grouse Inn at Carrog, just a short sojourn down the lane and over the river.

From the railway station walk back up the lane to the A5. On the opposite side of the road a stony streamside track is signed to Nant y Pandy and waymarked with a North Berwyn Way sign, the first of many you'll see throughout the day. At a junction ignore the left fork track, which climbs out of the valley, and stay with the track that passes through woodland close to the stream.

Beyond a cottage the route crosses a footbridge, after which a path continues along the west side of the stream, passing close to a second cottage before coming across the remains of the old slate works of Nant y Pandy Mill. Here the quarrymen would have cut blocks of slate excavated from the mid-level Deeside Slab Quarry into slabs used for gravestones, the brewing and building industry, and for operating tables for hospitals.

Hereabouts you're following part of an old tramway linking the slate mines of Moel Fferna with the old Ruabon to Barmouth railway at Glyndyfrdwy. Beyond some waterfalls the path re-crosses the stream on a slate bridge with wooden rails and soon joins a stony track, which passes two cottages. Where the track arcs right across fields leave it for a signed path on the left.

Below: One of the steam trains of the
Llangollen Railway, which calls at
Glyndyfrdwy and Carrog.

Above: Looking east along Moel Fferna ridge.

The woods have been left behind and you're in a moorland valley with a pastured side valley trending right towards the higher Deeside Slab Quarry and the heather moors beyond. A narrow path stays low at first through an area of bracken before climbing left to join a tarred lane. Turn right along this to reach the Moel Fferna–Vivod Mountain ridge, which here is topped with the conifers

of the Ceiriog Forest. On reaching the summit of the old road turn right on a heavily rutted track, which takes you alongside those conifers.

The track soon leaves the conifers behind and forges its way towards Moel Fferna, a rounded, rather dull-looking hill from here, but this will soon change as the landscape becomes wilder and more stimulating. On the left the sprawling crags of the high Berwyn ridge overlook the sultry heather slopes of the Ceiriog-ddu valley. A gaunt cluster of dead trees adds menace to the scene.

Stay with the ridge track, ignoring the North Berwyn Way sign which points downhill and right. Finally a right turn on a peaty path climbs to the wind-shelter on Moel Fferna's summit, from where there's an unbroken panorama of what seems like the whole of North Wales and the Cheshire/Shropshire borderlands. The sleek ridges of the Llantysilio and Clwydian lead the gaze westwards towards the bastions of northern Snowdonia while the Rhinogydd and Cadair Idris peaks take it further into the misty blue of Mid Wales.

Now the plan is to descend to Llidiart y Parc and neighbouring Carrog back in the Dee Valley. From the trig point a narrow path descends north-east down heather slopes to join the North Berwyn Way path by a marker post. Head north on an old grassy shooters' track, ignoring turn-offs to the right and left. The track descends to the right corner of a conifer plantation.

Enter the forest and head north quite close to its eastern boundary. The track is joined by one from the left, by some game-bird breeding pens, but shortly after is abandoned for a track forking left. This continues northwards for about a mile where you should watch out for a stepped path descending left. This crosses another track before descending further to the valley floor. The new track now takes the route north past a house, and more game-bird breeding pens.

It leads out to a tarred lane by Park Grove House, and this in turn leads to the A5 at Llidiart y Parc. Across the busy highway (cross with care) a lane leads down to the railway station, where I can heartily recommend you take the steam train to Glyndyfrdwy. Locals call it Glyn by the way, if you cannot get your tongue around the Welsh pronunciation when ordering tickets.

If you want more walking continue down the lane and cross the bridge over the Dee, where you may see lots of picnickers in summer, to the village of Carrog. The Grouse Inn is a superb pub if you need sustenance. Turn right at the T-junction and follow the pleasant country lane back to Glyndyfrdwy. There's a short stretch of riverside path near the start for those who have a little more time to spare.

Overleaf: The big Berwyn peaks seen from Fferna ridge.

MAPS

Ordnance Survey Explorer (1:25,000)
   OL 18 Snowdonia: Harlech,
   Porthmadog/Bala
   OL 23 Cadair Idris & Llyn Tegid
   Sheet 255 Llangollen & Berwyn
Ordnance Survey Landranger (1:50,000)
   Sheet 124 Porthmadog & Dolgellau
   Sheet 125 Bala & Lake Vyrnwy
Harveys Superwalker (1:25,000)
   Snowdonia: Snowdon and the
   Moelwynion
Harveys Snowdonia South British Mountain
   Map (1:40,000) covers much of this
   volume but not the Berwyn

TRANSPORT

Buses

Sherpa Buses, run by Gwynedd Council and Conwy County Borough Council with support from the Snowdonia National Park Authority, offer services in the Betws y Coed and Dolwyddelan areas, which is good for the hills around Cwm Penamnen and the Crimea Pass area above Blaenau Ffestiniog.

There's also a regular Arriva number 64 service from Llanrwst and Betws y Coed to the head of Cwm Penmachno via Penmachno village for walks up Y Ro Wen and Pen y Bedw. The Bala–Dolgellau X94 (Arriva) helps with routes to Dduallt and Rhobell Fawr and there's a bus service from Dolgellau to Llanfachreth for the same mountains.

Blaenau and Llan Ffestiniog are quite well served with buses so it's never too problematical to use public transport when walking the Moelwynion and Manod peaks. There's a regular service up the A470 from Dolgellau to Blaenau via Trawsfynydd.

In other parts services are sketchy. At present no bus connects Trawsfynydd and Bala so you're on your own with Arenig Fawr, Moel Llyfnant and the Migneint.

The Berwyn Mountains fare a little better. Regular buses, including the X94, go up and down the road from Wrexham to Bala via Llandrillo so the routes on northern and north-western ridges are well served,

and there are buses to Llanarmon Dyffryn
Ceiriog (Bryn Melyn). There's a spasmodic
D79 (Tanat Valley Coaches) service from
Oswestry and Chirk to Llanrhaeadr-ym-
mochnant and Llangynog, which helps
with routes from the south.

Bus timetables for the Conwy borough,
which includes Penmachno, Dolwyddelan
and Betws y Coed, are available twice
a year, either from TICs or by sending a
9 x 6in stamped addressed envelope to:
Conwy County Borough Council
Public Transport Section
Highways & Transportation Department
The Heath, Llanfairfechan LL33 0PF

Trains

There's a mainline railway linking
Llandudno, Betws-y-Coed and Blaenau
Ffestiniog – useful for routes around
Dolwyddelan and on the Moelwynion
range. The narrow-gauge Ffestiniog
Railway from Porthmadog to Blaenau
Ffestiniog via Tanygrisiau is excellent
for the Moelwynion and Manod peaks,
while the Llangollen railway now reaches
Carrog near Llidiart y Parc, and is good
for Moel Fferna. This will eventually be
extended to Corwen.

Rail travel timetable (Railtrack):
www.nationalrail.co.uk

For more information: www.traveline-
cymru.org.uk

Tourist information Centres (year round)
Bala
    Tel. 01678 521021
    Email: bala.tic@gwynedd.gov.uk
Betws y Coed
    Tel. 01690 710426
    Email: tic.byc@eryri-npa.gov.uk
Blaenau Ffestiniog
    Tel. 01766 830360
    Email: tic.blaenau@eryri-npa.gov.uk
Dolgellau
    Tel. 01341 422888
    Email: tic.dolgellau@eryri-npa.gov.uk
Llangollen
    Tel. 01341 280787
    Email: barmouth.tic@gwynedd.gov.uk

Websites
Welsh Tourist Board: www.visitwales.com
Snowdonia Information:
    www.visitsnowdonia.info
Accommodation: www.4tourism.com

BEST BASES

Bala Bala is very central for much of the region and has a good deal of accommodation ranging from a private hostel, several campsites, through to fine hotels and country houses. It has a small gear shop, and a couple of supermarkets.

Betws y Coed This large and bustling village is set by an equally bustling river, the Llugwy, not far from its confluence with the Afon Conwy. Betws has scores of B&Bs and many hotels. It's a good place for renewing supplies, with a choice of grocers, bakers, and several gear shops. It within striking distance of the northern Ffestiniog range and the north-eastern Arenig and Migneint peaks.

Corwen Always in the shadows of both Llangollen and Bala, Corwen has smartened itself up lately. There is a fine country house hotel, Bron-y-graig (sometimes referred to as Edge House), and a couple of inns. There are shops for restocking although no gear shops at present. Nearby Carrog has one of the best pubs in North Wales, the Grouse Inn.

Dolgellau Although it is sited beneath Cadair Idris some way south of the region, Dolgellau is reasonably placed for the southern Arenig peaks. The charming country town has hotels and B&Bs, and is well served by public transport.

Dolwyddelan In the heart of the Lledr Valley, scenic Dolwyddelan is famous for its hilltop castle. With a couple of inns and B&Bs and a campsite, and accessible by railway and bus, it is ideal for Y Ro Wen, Moel Penamnen and Moelwynion peaks.

Llanarmon Dyffryn Ceiriog Set deep in the verdant Ceiriog Valley, this is one of the prettiest villages in Wales. Two ancient coaching inns face each other across the town square. Unfortunately there are no shops or campsites. You'll need a car for most routes but many of the narrow country lanes do take you into the heart of the Berwyn mountains.

Llandrillo On the banks of the Dee, with a spired church, two restaurants, B&Bs and campsites, Llandrillo is a fine base for exploring the north-western Berwyn.

Llangollen This large, bustling, picturesque village is famous throughout the world for its eisteddfods, but it's also an excellent base for the Berwyn mountains. The plentiful hotels, B&Bs, youth hostel and campsites all add up to plenty of accommodation. The Chain Bridge Hotel, which is shoehorned into a narrow isthmus between the River Dee and the Llangollen Canal, is one of the most romantically sited hotels in the area.

Llan Ffestiniog This most beautiful of Welsh villages has come under hard times of late, which is sad, for it's sited on a verdant pastoral shelf overlooking the vale of the same name and has striking mountain and coastal views. There are two waterfalls nearby within walking distance of the local B&B. The village is well placed for the western Migneint and Ffestiniog Hills.

Llangynog Once a thriving lead mining resort and terminus of the Tanat Valley Railway, Llangynog now caters for the mountain tourist intent on spending time on the Berwyn mountains. There are two inns and a campsite.

Porthmadog This busy resort, sited at the mouth of the Glaslyn Estuary, has accommodation to suit all tastes, ranging from hotels – including a Travelodge – to B&Bs and campsites. There is a large supermarket, several cafés and many specialist shops. Nearby Tremadog, a climbers' centre, has a few inns, a fish and chip shop and a village store. Well-known climber Eric Jones runs a café, bunkbarn and a campsite for tents just east of Tremadog (tel. 01766 512199).

Betws y Coed
Swallow Falls, Betws Y Coed LL24 0DW
Tel. 01690 710796
Email: betwsycoed@yha.org.uk

Dolgellau (Penmaenpool)
Kings, Penmaenpool LL40 1TB
Tel. 0845 371 9327
Email: kings@yha.org.uk

YHA National Office
Trevelyan House, Dimple Road, Matlock, Derbyshire DE4 3YH
Tel. 0870 770 8868
Website: www.yha.org.uk

THE WELSH LANGUAGE

Some Welsh words

aber	river mouth
afon	river
arddu	black crag
bach/fach	small
bedd	grave
betws	chapel
blaen	head of valley
bont/pont	bridge
bwlch	pass
bws	bus
cae	field
caer	fort
carn/carnedd/garn/garnedd	cairn/cairns
capel	chapel
carreg/garreg	stone
castell	castle
cefn	ridge
cors/gors	bog
clogwyn	cliff
coch/goch	red
coeden/coed	tree/wood
craig/graig	crag
crib	sharp ridge
cwm	coomb
cwn	dog
Cymru/Cymraeg	Wales/Welsh
dinas	hill fort (or town)
diolch	thank you
du/ddu	black
drum/trum	ridge
drws	door
dyffryn	valley
dwr	water
eglwys	church
esgair	ridge
eryri	eagles' abode
fawr/mawr	large
felin/melin	mill
ffordd	road
ffynnon	spring
ffridd	enclosed grazing land
glas/las	blue
gwrydd	green
gwyn	white
gwynt	wind
hafod	high-altitude summer dwelling
hendre	winter dwelling
isaf	lower
llan	church or blessed place
llwybr cyhoeddus	public footpath
llwyd	grey
llyn	lake
maen	stone
maes	field/meadow
melyn	yellow
moch	pig
moel/foel	featureless hill
mynydd	mountain
nant	stream
ogof	cave
pant	clearing, hollow
pen	peak
person	cascade
plas	mansion
pwll	pool
rhaeadr	waterfall
rhyd	ford

saeth(au)	arrow(s)
troed	foot of
twll	hole, fracture, broken
ty	house
uchaf	high, higher
waun	moor
wen	white
wrach	witch
y, yr	the
ynys	island

Pronunciation of consonants

c	always hard, like the English 'k', thus coed = 'koyd'
ch	as in the Scottish 'loch'
dd	a voiced 'th' as in 'booth'
f	like the English 'v' , thus fach = 'vach'
ff	like the English 'f'
ll	a Scots 'ch' followed by an 'l' (blow air out between your tongue and your top teeth when pronouncing)

Pronunciation of vowels

w	can be a consonant or a vowel. When working as a vowel, pronounced like 'oo' as in 'cook' or 'moon'.
y	can be a consonant or a vowel. When working as a vowel, pronounced like 'i' as in pin or 'ee' as in seen. U is exactly the same.

The letters j, k, q, v, x and z are not used in true Welsh words.